His Life Is In
THE BLOOD

APMI Publications
a division of Kingdom Dimension Books
P.O. Box 17,
55051 Barga (LU),
Tuscany, Italy

His Life Is In
THE BLOOD

DR. ALAN PATEMAN

BOOK TITLE:
His Life is in the Blood

This edition published in 2017

Published by APMI Publications
A Division of Kingdom Dimension Books, Library No. **4**
P.O. Box 17,
55051 Barga (LU),
Italy

Email: publications@alanpatemanworldmissions.com
www.AlanPatemanWorldMissions.com

**APMI Publications and Kingdom Dimension Books are a division of
Alan Pateman World Missions**

Printed in the United States of America, Europe and Asia

Paperback ISBN: 978-1-909132-06-1
eBook ISBN: 978-0-9570654-1-3

Acknowledgements:
Author/Design/Senior Editor/Publisher: Apostle Dr. Alan Pateman
Editing/Proofreading/Research: Dr. Jennifer Pateman
Computer Administration/Office Manager: Dr. Dorothea Struhlik
Cover Image Credit: © jc_cards www.fotolia.com

Unless otherwise indicated, all scriptural quotations are from the HOLY BIBLE, NEW INTERNATIONAL VERSION ®. NIV ®. Copyright © 1973, 1978, 1984 by the International Bible Society. Used by permission of Zondervan Publishing House. All rights reserved.

*Where scriptures appear with special emphasis (**in bold,** italic or <u>underlined</u>) we have edited them ourselves in order to bring focused attention within the context of this subject being taught.*

❖

Dedication

I would like to dedicate this book to my wife Jenny. It must be said that without her support, especially her love and understanding, my task in writing this book and others would take far longer and be practically more difficult. I rely heavily on her typing skills, which she so willingly volunteers to help me with the books that God has commissioned me to write.

She not only juggles her responsibilities, which all wives and mothers have, but also gives of her time, which very often takes us into the small hours! Thank you for the many hours of editing, typing and other contributions you have given to this book.

❖

Table of Contents

❖

Introduction

In the wake of September 11, 2001, when the world arose to the terror inflicted by a series of coordinated terrorist suicide attacks by a group of well-organized extremists, words could not express the shock and disbelief of such a catastrophe. Of course, this type of devastation is actually happening in many parts of the world with the increase of wars and political rumors of such, just as the Scriptures predict.

We could write several books about the *miscarriages of justice* inflicted by governments and their regimes, not forgetting that many political groups now considered politically respectable, started off as terrorists themselves!

But what we are concerned with here is the unbelievable shock of witnessing thousands of innocent people dying **live** on CNN under the clear blue early morning sky of 9/11, in New York's throbbing metropolis.

Destruction came at the hands of 19 Islamic extremists, whose plan of *hijack and attack* upon America unfolded before our very eyes as we witnessed the unprecedented destruction of the multiple towers of the *World Trade Centre* complex, causing approximately three thousand deaths – the victims being predominantly civilian *(see www.wikipedia. com)*.

Then there was the plane that went into the Pentagon. The incredibly heroic actions of the passengers on *United Flight 93* prevented yet another flying bomb from hitting more strategic targets, such as any of the five nuclear power plants 150 miles northwest of Washington!

This attack did not merely bring about death, but also psychological and emotional pain for thousands of partners, husbands and wives, not to mention the children who were left bereft of mothers or fathers. Then came the wave of fear that assailed people in the following months, to the point that people were not willing to step outside their own homes, after having witnessed such devastating carnage.

Thereafter followed loss of jobs; the landslide of stock market losses; massive retail and manufacturing losses; failed businesses due to inevitable bankruptcies; and even the losses of personal wealth. It has been said that even Osama Bin Laden himself was astonished by what he had initiated through these attacks!

There was no warning of these sudden acts of terrorism. No one saw it coming – to the supposed embarrassment of

America. *But now everyone is on alert for the unthinkable to happen!*

In reflection, the response from the rest of the world to those atrocities was unbelievably positive in the sense of *our wake-up call.* The call reminded us that evil exists and that terror is an increasing reality, especially in our so-called sophisticated and well-organized world.

Humanistically, of course, the world quickly moved on. It cosmetically overcame, but finds itself changed, having to deal with this growing threat continually. It is clear, there will be **no end** or decline to terrorism, as it is not a trend and will not dissipate. It is part of end-time spiritual warfare, as predicted in Scripture, that steadily increases, rather than wanes, as some suppose.

The increase of technology only increases these threats! The perpetrators and organizers are still at large, living as international fugitives on the one hand and religious heroes on the other. Evading every attempt of capture, while continuing to gather countless new recruits, increasing in numbers and expertise, they are highly organized, highly trained, highly armed and highly funded by heavyweights who stand to gain politically.

In 2001 we witnessed *the awakening of the Great Tiger from its slumber!* As a result, we also saw America, with its allies *(mainly England),* attempt to chase terror back to its roots throughout the world – a massive, costly and largely unpopular undertaking. Afghanistan was brought to its knees in response for harboring Osama Bin Laden, although at this time (2001), he is still at large.

Then it was Iraq's turn, with the invasion of Iraq and the downfall of Saddam Hussein. His eventual verdict was *death by hanging,* after an arduous year in court, which Saddam and his lackeys repeatedly accused as illegitimate, mocking the whole legal process as a political farce!

The world witnessed as the combative Hussein defiantly and persistently refused to accept the authority of the court. Nevertheless, the final verdict was eventually met by Iraqis on the street with mixed reactions of jubilation and protest!

Policing the world is of course an impossible task, yet it is clearly possible for those powers that be to arise at their own discretion or will in response to aggression, regardless of who is pushing the buttons.

However, this book is not majoring on end-time events such as *War On Terror* by Dr Grant Jeffrey or *Jerusalem Countdown* by John Hagee *(strongly suggested readings),* but on questions that all humanity is asking right now:

- What is this life on planet earth all about?
- What purpose does such devastation have?
- How does this affect me?
- Am I in danger?

Fear is the **tormentor** *or terrorist of the unregenerate soul.* What I mean is this: anyone without a spiritual foundation or understanding will never be able to comprehend or come to terms with these increasingly dramatic end-time world events.

Introduction

For America, especially, our hearts went out to all the victims of 9/11 and those who suffered in the repercussions. Nevertheless, we also know that it resulted in millions who arrived at the realization of their **urgent need to get right with their Maker.**

9/11 did serve as a huge wake-up call for many, not only America, exposing the whole world to its dire apathy and complacency in life. It also showed how easy it is to be lulled into a false sense of security by the cosmetics and superficialities of life!

Shallow politics and news reels that consist only of *fluff and stuff (fake news)* create the impression that all is well with the propaganda machine, while allowing death, torment and fear to go on the rampage undetected.

I sincerely believe that revelation will be ignited in your heart as you turn the pages of *His Life Is In The Blood* and that it will help you find the answers to some of the heart-wrenching questions that we've all asked at one stage or another.

Understanding is so desperately needed. Proverbs 4:7 KJV says: *With all thy getting get understanding.*

Be secure! You are not alone when you ask, *Why did this happen and can it happen to me?* So receive the revelation contained in this book – inspired by the Holy Spirit – and remember above all that, ***His Life is in the Blood.***

Dr Alan Pateman

❖

CHAPTER 1

God's Perfect Love

The Price is Paid

We begin by referring to the perfect Love of God, revealed to us by the price that was paid for each and every one of us; the very precious **Blood** of His Son.

Dear friends, let us love one another, for love comes from God. Everyone who loves has been born of God and knows God. Whoever does not love does not know God, because God is love.

*This is how **God showed his love among us: He sent his one and only Son into the world that we might live through him.** This is love: not that we loved God, but that he loved us and sent his Son as an atoning sacrifice for our sins.*

(1 John 4:7-10)

I think it has to be said that the majority of the Body of Christ doesn't really understand the profound **Love** of God; the divine initiative called *reconciliation*. Any love you show Him is only a response to His divine love with which He first loved you *(John 3:3, 3:16; Romans 3:22-26)*.

He took the first step towards you through the ultimate Love act, which was to send His one and only Son to die as final atonement for your personal sins.

Jesus Picked Up The Check
Debt Is Written Off

The offering up of Himself was the ultimate and most perfect of all offerings which satisfied the justice of God. Only on the grounds of that sacrifice can God the Father accept you as His own and judge you **innocent** for eternity.

Died in Your Place

Without Christ we were unrighteous and had no hope of ever being righteous outside of the cross. Our only hope was Christ, who failed us not, stepping into our shoes and suffering the penalty for our crime. Even without sin, He suffered the punishment due a sinner – the Law's requirement.

Righteousness willingly took the place of unrighteousness; only through Christ can the unrighteous and the righteous trade places! Jesus nailed unrighteousness to the cross, and through His righteousness we were made right before God.

For Christ died for sins once for all, the righteous for the unrighteous, to bring you to God. He was put to death in the body but made alive by the Spirit.

(1 Peter 3:18)

No Obstacle Stands in the Way

After His death on the cross, the veil in the temple was torn in two. Any separation from God experienced before the cross has now been dealt with through the eternal **Blood Covenant** ratified on Calvary's Tree; for those accepting the reality of Christ *(see Romans 1:16).*

*But their minds were made dull, for to this day the same veil remains when the old covenant is read. It has not been removed, because **only in Christ is it taken away.***

(2 Corinthians 3:14)

Access was given because of the **Blood;** access to the throne of love, mercy and grace. Calling Jehovah *Father* remained impossible without the pure **Blood** of Christ.

In fact, every single time salvation occurs for an individual, the veil is taken away instantly!

Whenever anyone turns to the Lord, the veil is taken away. *Now the Lord is the Spirit, and where the Spirit of the Lord is, there is freedom.*

(2 Corinthians 3:16-17)

Only when one **turns** *(through repentance)*, can individual veils be lifted. The washing of the **Blood** cleanses, which allows the Spirit of God's Holiness to come in; only then can we experience true **freedom.** Freedom from the bondage of sin and death, freedom to live in Christ and for Christ, freedom to be a child of God and freedom to worship Him *in spirit and in truth (John 4:24).*

Amazing Love Has Set This Captive Free!

Death is Conquered, Victory Secure!

Jesus shared our humanity *completely.* Temptation was not far from Him, yet He never sinned. Death He tasted, but not for Himself. In fact, He had no reason to die, were it just for Himself, because He was **without sin** *(2 Corinthians 5:21).*

The only reason Christ died was for the sake of humanity – who were the true recipients of punishment worthy of death, because of their sins against God.

> *Since the children have flesh and blood, he too* **shared in their humanity** *so that by his death he might destroy him who holds the power of death – that is, the devil - and free those who all their lives were held in slavery by their fear of death.*
>
> *(Hebrews 2:14-15)*

Judgement rested heavily upon humanity and could not be averted. Sin had to be punished by death; **blood** had to be shed. Our God is merciful, but He is also **just.** Jesus satisfied every requirement; dying a *sinless* death.

Eternal separation was the verdict passed against humanity – but Jesus appealed on the grounds of His **Blood** and won the case – *which will never be overruled! (see Isaiah 9:7)*

The End Of Fear

Infirmity no Longer has a Hold

Isaiah prophesied Jesus' victory over disease and sickness:

This was to fulfil what was spoken through the prophet Isaiah: **"He took up our infirmities and carried our diseases."**

(Matthew 8:17)

In Matthew chapter 4 verse 24 it says that Jesus healed all who were brought to Him. During His ministry on earth, Jesus demonstrated the Father's love by healing their infirmities. Love desires that *none should perish but have everlasting life (John 3:16).*

The condition of our spirit, soul and body is of importance to God *(1 Thessalonians 5:23).* Jesus didn't merely take our sin to the cross, but also our infirmities and diseases. *By his wounds we are healed (Isaiah 53:5).*

John 4:34 says that Jesus came to do the will of the Father; *to do the will of Him who sent me.* It is the Father's will that you be saved and healed and that you receive every spiritual blessing *(Ephesians 1:3-14).*

Jesus did all that was necessary to see that the will of His Father was fulfilled; *...and to* **finish** *His work.* That's why Jesus could declare from the cross before He died, *It is* **finished** *(John 19:30).*

The Work Of The Cross Is Complete
Spirit, Soul And Body

Risen for Us

When all was accomplished, Jesus ascended to His Father's side, yet there was no closure! His work continues! He lives forever to minister in the presence of God on our behalf; interceding for us continually *(see Romans 8:34).*

And when God the Father sees Jesus, He sees us, as we are *...seated in heavenly places* **in** *Christ Jesus (Ephesians 2:6).* Imagine this: if the Father sees Christ continually before His face, we are also seen continually! Each time He sees us, He sees Christ; each time He sees Christ, He sees us. **Reconciled forever;** eternally found **in** Christ Jesus.

> **Who shall separate us** *from the love of Christ? Shall trouble or hardship...?*
>
> *(Romans 8:35)*

So, God the Father always sees us **together!** Under the **Blood,** nothing can separate us! When He looks upon us, He not only sees us or Christ but He also sees His **Covenant.** We are eternal reminders, found continually before His throne – **in Christ Jesus.**

That's why Romans 8:1-4 says that the only ones who are free from condemnation are those who are **in Christ Jesus.** Those in condemnation *(of the flesh)* cannot stand before the throne of God, only those who are **in Christ Jesus,** *...according to the Spirit.*

Outside of Christ we look like **sin,** but **in Christ** we actually look like Him!

We Used To Look Like Sin
Now We Look Like Him!

You Will Never be Denied

Because Jesus is your faithful High Priest, who *...lives always to intercede for you,* according to Hebrews 7:25, you will never be denied when you enter into God's presence. This free passage and unlimited access to the throne afforded you by the cross, allows you unrestrained favor before God; as long as you **remain in Christ.**

Jesus underwent such terrible suffering, for a special purpose, and that was to make us holy, as He is holy *(1 Peter 1:16).*

*Jesus...**suffered...to make the people holy** through his own **Blood.***

(Hebrews 13:12)

He Suffered To Make Us Holy

His Ever Faithful Love

God is the same yesterday, today and forever, and there is no shadow of turning with Him. His love remains constant throughout the generations.

Because we witnessed the faithfulness of Christ towards His Father – staying true to His will under all circumstances

– we know that without failure or compromise Jesus will remain faithful to us! He is unable to change, He forever remains the same. His Love has been tested and proven to be **unconditional!**

It all rests on who **He is,** as 1 John 4:7-21 declares, *God is Love,* and 1 Corinthians 13:8 reminds us that *Love never fails.*

God's love is **never** based on anything we have done. It is only ever based upon what Jesus accomplished, for yesterday, today and forever.

"I think that if there could be one sight more wonderful than the Love of Christ," said Charles H. Spurgeon, *"it would be the **Blood** of Christ."*

So Much Talk Of His Blood
Yet So Little Is Understood!

Spurgeon goes on to say, "I do not know of anything more divine. It seems to me as if all the eternal purposes worked up to the Blood of the Cross, and then worked from the **Blood** of the cross towards the sublime consummation of all things. Oh, to think that He should become man!

God has made spirit, pure spirit, embodied spirit; and then materialism; and somehow, as if He would take all up into one, the Godhead links Himself with the material.

He then wears dust about Him even as we wear it; and taking it all up, He then goes, and in that fashion, redeems His people from all the evil of their soul, their spirit, and their body, by the pouring out of a life, which while it was human, was so in connection with the divine, that we speak correctly of 'the **Blood** of God.'

Turn to the twentieth chapter of the Acts, and read how the apostle Paul puts it: *'Feed the church of God, which he hath purchased with his own* **Blood**.' I believe that Dr. Watts is not wrong when he says – *'God that loved and died.'* **It is an incorrect accuracy, a strictly absolute accuracy of incorrectness!**

So it must be ever when the finite talks of the Infinite. It was a wonderful sacrifice that could absolutely obliterate, annihilate, and extinguish sin, and all the traces that could possibly remain of it; for *'He hath finished the transgression, made an end of sins, made reconciliation for iniquity, and brought in everlasting righteousness.'*

Ah, dear friends! You have seen this, have you not? But you have to see more of it yet; and when we get to heaven, we shall then know what that **Blood** means, and with what vigour shall we sing...

He Loved Us And
Washed Us In His Own Blood!

Will anybody be there to say, *'Is not that the religion of shambles?'* as they blasphemously call it?

Ah, my friends! **They will find themselves where they will wish they had believed 'the religion of shambles.'** I think that it will burn like coals of juniper into the soul of any man that has ever dared to talk like that, that he did despite the **Blood** of God, and so, by his own wilful deeds, will be cast away forever.

May the Holy Spirit show unto you Gethsemane, and Gabbatha, and Golgotha! And then, may it please Him to give you a sight of what our Lord is now doing! Oh, *how it would cheer you up at any time* when you were depressed, only *to see Him standing and pleading for you!*

Do you not think that if your wife is ill, and your child is sick, and there is scant food in the cupboard, if you were to go out at the back door, and saw Him with the breast-plate on, and all the stones glittering, and your name there, and Him pleading for you, you would go in and say, *'There, wife, it is all right. He is praying for us?'*

Oh, it would be a comfort if the Holy Ghost showed you a pleading Christ! *And then, to think that He is reigning as well as pleading.* He is at the right hand of God, even the Father, who hath put all things under His feet. And He waits till the last enemy shall lie there.

Now, you are not afraid, are you, of those who have said, *'All power is given unto me in heaven and in earth. Go ye therefore, and teach all nations; and lo, I am with you always, even unto the end of the world.'*

Next, and best of all, may the Holy Spirit give you a clear view of His coming. This is our most brilliant hope: *'Lo, He cometh!'* The more the adversary waxes bold, and the less of faith there is, and when zeal seems almost extinct, these are the tokens of his coming. The Lord always said so; and that He would not come unless there was a falling away first.

So the darker the night grows, and the fiercer the storm becomes, the better will we remember that He at the lake of

Galilee came to them upon the waves in the night when the storm was wildest. Oh, what will His enemies say when He comes?

He Came When The
Storm Was At Its Wildest!

When they behold the nail-prints of the Glorified, and the man with the thorn crown – when they see Him really come – they that have despised his word, and his ever-blessed *Blood, how will they flee before that face of injured love!*

And we on the contrary, through His infinite mercy, will say, *'This is what the Holy Ghost showed us; and now we behold it literally. We thank Him for the foresights which He gave us of the beatific vision.'*

I have not done on the first head yet, because there is one point which I want you to recollect. When the Holy Ghost takes of the things of Christ, and shows them to us, He has a purpose in so doing. It is with you, with regard to the Spirit showing you things, as it was with Jacob.

You know Jacob lay down, and went to sleep, and the Lord said to him, *'The land whereon thou liest, to thee will I give it.'* Now,wherever you go, throughout the whole of Scripture, *if you can sleep on a promise, that promise is yours.*

If You Can Sleep On A Promise
That Promise Is Yours

'Lift up now thine eyes,' said God to Abraham, *'and look from the place where thou are northward, and southward, and eastward, and westward: for all the land, which thou seest, to thee will I give it.'*

The Lord increase our holy vision of delighted faith; *for there is nothing you see but you may also enjoy; all that is in Christ is there for you"* (Morgan and Spurgeon 345-347).

❖

CHAPTER 2

Raised to New Life

Living in Christ

J esus took not only our sin to the cross, but us as well! According to the Scriptures, *we died with Him.* And because of this, we can also *live with Him,* not just in this life on earth, but for eternity. We died with Him – and by faith we now **live** with Him and **in** Him **forever!**

Now if we died with Christ, we believe that we will also live with him.

(Romans 6:8)

Crucified with Christ

Like Paul the apostle we are permitted to say:

I have been crucified with Christ and I no longer live, but Christ lives in me. The life I live in the body,

I live by faith in the Son of God, who loved me and gave himself for me.

(Galatians 2:20)

Jesus took your old sin nature to the cross, then replaced it with His Divine Nature *(see 2 Peter 1:4)*. Now, like Paul, we live by *...faith in the Son of God.* Our inheritance is Christ Jesus Himself – all that He is – plus what He has made available: *...Every spiritual blessing (Ephesians 1:3).*

*Blessed be the God and Father of our Lord Jesus Christ, who has **blessed us with every spiritual blessing** in the heavenly places **in Christ...***

(Ephesians 1:3 NKJ)

We no longer have to rely on our own limited and simple finite resources of power and strength, but on the infinite power of the Trinity, which is infused and invested within us.

*For we know that our **old self was crucified with him** so that the **body of sin** might be done away with, that we should no longer be slaves to sin – because anyone who has died has been freed [cleared] from sin.*

(Romans 6:6-7)

The old life has been crucified that the *...body of sin might be done away with.* Notice the inclusion of the word **might.** This is due to the decision that you and I must make daily to *take up our cross **daily*** and to follow Him *(Matthew 10:38).*

The self-life has to be done away with daily. Constantly we have to contend with our own flesh, as we are **in** the flesh but not **of** it. We must continually resist the ungodly lusts and desires of this *earth-suit* while we walk this planet!

There's a War going On!

As the apostle Peter told the early believers, *...abstain from fleshly lusts which **war against the soul...** (1 Peter 2:11)* or like James said, *...desires for pleasure that war in your members.*

This inner war of cravings and selfish desires never ceases, striving to entangle us in the flesh, rather than allowing us to follow hard after the Spirit.

Romans 8:1,13 says: *Do not walk according to the flesh, but according to the Spirit... if you live according to the flesh you will die; but if by the Spirit... you will live (see also Galatians 6:8; Romans 7; Galatians 5:16; 1 John 2:16; Romans 13:14; Titus 2:12; 1 Peter 1:14; Jude 18).*

Warring against our Soul

The death and resurrection of Christ won the ultimate victory; nevertheless, we must deliberately enforce that victory over our lives daily. It takes choice and unrelenting discipline to walk in resurrection victory.

Our position is strong and secure; Christ won an irrevocable victory and made us more than conquerors. However, we must continue on that path of righteousness, in willing cooperation *(see Isaiah 1:19).*

Paul likened our walk with Christ to a person who enters an athletic competition. Every contestant has the ability to disqualify himself, through several possibilities, such as simply not starting well, or not turning up on time, or quitting at any stage of the course, either due to fatigue or lack of morale. *(We could say lack of preparation, fitness, stamina or spiritual strength, such as longsuffering!)*

Any *unethical behavior* would also disqualify that person, even an unwitting error, such as taking the wrong route or accidentally injuring another contestant. There are many ways in which to disqualify oneself, even in spiritual things. Nevertheless, it is important to note that every contestant must be qualified just to **enter** the race, never mind to start!

Christ is our entry! Christ qualified us, but to remain qualified, we must remain in Him, just as one must remain in a race. Sadly, many begin well: they start in the spirit, but end in the flesh!

It is evident to conclude that every entered contestant must see that race through without being disqualified for any reason. It takes more than inspiration to see a challenge through; inspiration alone wears thin rapidly! We need longevity and commitment *(spiritual stamina and character)*.

Every Qualified Entry Was A Volunteer

It's the flesh that *disqualifies* us. We must allow our flesh-life to be *"done away with"* and continually walk according to the Spirit and not the flesh. **Jesus died to give us this legal privilege** *(see Romans 8:2)*.

Does Grace declare: Once saved Always saved?

Yes, there is **grace!** We are saved by grace and not by works. We know what is undeserved can never be **earned!** Christ's **Blood** was shed for us deliberately. He will **never** reverse His decision to save. The work of the cross is complete. However, it **is** possible for us to reverse our decision to *follow* and *obey* the Lord of our lives. He is **Lord,** not just Savior – we are His disciples, not mere converts.

God's step towards us was perfect and pure in motive. However, the Bible says we only love Him because He first loved us. Jesus was given that none should perish. Oh, for the beautiful grace that saved us! Grace was sufficient for Christ, even under trial and temptation, and it is sufficient for us today.

With the help of His Holy Spirit, we will complete this race without quitting. The Holy Spirit is our Helper, advocate, confidant and support; our **holy stamina** to fulfil this race. It is our prerogative not only to **start** in the Spirit, but to **end** in the Spirit!

> *Not by might nor by power, but by my Spirit, says the Lord of hosts.*
>
> *(Zechariah 4:6)*

Only Dead People are FREE!

*We know that our old (unrenewed) self was nailed to the cross with Him in order that [our] body [which is the instrument] of sin might be made ineffective and inactive for evil, that we might no longer be the slaves of sin. **For when a man dies, he is freed** (loosed, delivered) from [the power of] sin [among men].*

(Romans 6:6-7 AMP)

When we are dead to the flesh, sin no longer has the mastery over us. We are no longer controlled by sin. Jesus broke the power of sin over our lives and we have been transferred *...from the law of sin and death...* to *...the law of the Spirit of life in Christ Jesus (Romans 8:1-2).* It is the Holy Spirit who helps us to *...put to death the deeds of the body (Romans 8:13).*

However, because sin still exists, temptation is never far away. But we no longer need to yield to the compulsion to sin and disobey the Lord. Instead, we can yield to the Holy Spirit and declare our Freedom in Christ Jesus. We are partakers of His death **and** resurrection. By the Spirit we can count ourselves **dead** to sin and **alive** in Christ!

No Longer Yielding To Temptation
No Longer Slaves To Sin

Baptized into His Death

*Are you ignorant of the fact that **all of us who have been baptized into Christ Jesus were baptized into His death?** We were buried therefore with Him by the **baptism into death,** so that just as Christ was raised from the dead by the glorious [power] of the Father, so we too might [habitually] live and behave in newness of life.*

*For if we have become one with Him by **sharing a death like His, we shall also be [one with Him in sharing] His resurrection** [by a new life lived for God]. We know that our old (unrenewed) self was nailed to the cross with Him in order that [our] body [which is the instrument] of* *sin might be made ineffective and inactive for evil, that we might no longer be the slaves of sin.*

Now if we have died with Christ, we believe that we shall also live with Him. *Because we know that Christ (the Anointed One), being once raised from the dead, will never die again; death no longer has power over Him. Even so **consider yourselves also dead to sin** and your relation to it broken, but [that you are] alive to God [living in unbroken fellowship with Him] in Christ Jesus.*
(Romans 6:3-6,8,9,11 AMP)

The old **you** is dead and gone... never to be resurrected! In fact, when you were baptized, it signified your choice not only to be slain with Christ but also to rise again, to live a new life in Him. Everything of your old *self-life* has passed away. **Yet newness of life belongs to you in the resurrected Christ,** who rose so that you also could be resurrected into a **new life** of victory!

God no longer sees your old nature, but the new one, which He so graciously and freely gave to you – and **it's important for all of us to see ourselves in this light –** *just as the Father sees us!*

There is power in this new nature of ours. Where the power of sin and death once ruled, the power of the resurrection now reigns in us through the Holy Spirit, who helps us to become all that God intends us to be. *Thanks be to God for ever more!*

Free To Walk In The Power Of Our New Nature

Hidden with Christ

*For [as far as this world is concerned] you have died, and your [new, real] life is **hidden with Christ in God.***
(Colossians 3:3 AMP)

The life we are now meant to live is *...hidden with Christ in God*. Because we died with Him, we can also **live** with Him.

No longer is our existence identified by our old unregenerate carnal nature, *[with its animal impulses... Colossians 3:5 AMP]*, instead, our lives are identified and located in Christ, which means our personal identities are completely rapped up in Jesus.

Christ lives with the Father in complete and perfect unity, a privilege that now also belongs to us! Only because we chose to die with Christ can we also claim to be risen with Him, our lives now *...hidden with Christ in God*.

Christ Lives In You
And You In Him!

Dead to This World

You have died with Christ to material ways of looking at things and have escaped from the world's crude and elemental notions and teachings of externalism.
(Colossians 2:20 AMP)

Carnal thinking and worldly living are privileges of the flesh, in which you can no longer indulge yourself! Undeniably we have not been raised to *Newness of Life* only to conform once again to this age. Indeed not! Instead, we are progressively being transformed by the continual renewing of our minds.

Having considered this new life, *...hidden with Christ in God,* and its joyous consequences, we must also consider its awesome responsibilities! We are responsible to develop a lifestyle totally dependent on God and totally surrendered to His Holy Spirit, only then can we make a *holy impact* upon the lives of others.

Yet, even as we attempt to live holy lives **before** God and **with** God, we will continually face challenges and temptations. But Colossians 2:20 says we have *...died with Christ from the basic principles of the world.*

We cannot continue in the mindset of the world or in carnality. Our citizenship is of heaven, not of this present world. We remain **in** this world but not **of** it. Our standards are higher – from the very Kingdom of God.

The values we live by are those exemplified in the Lord Jesus Christ, those of His life, those of His Word. Values based on all that He is.

However, the basic principles of this world which Colossians talks about such as selfishness, pleasure seeking, self-pity, self-gratification, self-sufficiency, self-praise, self-seeking, self-exaltation, self-concern, self-love, **self and more self,** can only result in a lifestyle of self-worship!

But you and I, the **Blood**-purchased children of God, **not only reject this way of life, but have literally died to this**

way of life. We have died to the self-focusing, self-absorbed and self-possessed nature of this world *(see Galatians 6:14).*

We Have Died To Worldly Principles And Obsession With Self

Dead to the Law

> *You also have become **dead to the law** through the body of Christ, that you may be married to another, even to Him who was raised from the dead, **that we should bear fruit to God.***
>
> *(Romans 7:4 NKJ)*

The Law could not bear fruit, because the law could never produce New Life. No religious system can bring new life; only life in Christ by the Holy Spirit can bear fruit for our Father. Jesus said in John 15 that the Father is glorified when we bear *...much fruit (verse 8).* Not **small,** not **some,** but **much** fruit.

> **We know that a man is justified** *or reckoned righteous and in right standing with God* **not by works of the Law, but** *[only]* **through faith** *and [absolute] reliance on and adherence to and trust* **in Jesus Christ** *(the Messiah, the Anointed One).*
>
> *[Therefore] even we [ourselves] have believed on Christ Jesus, in order to be justified by faith in Christ and not by works of the Law [for **we cannot be justified by any observance of the ritual of the Law** given by Moses], because* **by keeping legal rituals and by works no**

human being can ever be justified (declared righteous
and put in right standing with God).
(Galatians 2:16 AMP)

Anyone relying on religious duties or formats, instead of
simple faith in Jesus Christ, will inevitably have to admit that
all their efforts *to do and be right* will never be enough! **Self-
effort is exhausting, unfulfilling, frustrating and fruitless.**
Only a life lived by the Word and the Holy Spirit can ever
bear the kind of fruit that the Father is looking for.

A Life Of Fruitfulness For God

Free from Condemnation

*Therefore, [there is] now **no condemnation** [no adjudging
guilty of wrong) for those who are in Christ Jesus, who
live [and] walk not after the dictates of the flesh, but after
the dictates of the Spirit. For **the law of the Spirit of life**
[which is] in Christ Jesus [the law of our new being] **has
freed me from the law of sin and of death.***
(Romans 8:1-2 AMP)

God is not a God of anger but of **Love!** And He looks
upon us with love. *If we are in Christ we have no fear of
judgement.* As we permit the Lordship of the Holy Spirit
in our lives *(2 Corinthians 3:17; Romans 8:1b-2)*, who always
leads us into full obedience to Christ, then we will have no
fear of the coming judgement.

But, for those who refuse to walk in Christ by the Holy
Spirit, things are not so secure! In fact, they bring judgement
upon themselves. However, God desires that none should

perish, as He is not bent on punishment, but on **forgiveness and love.**

Although God's character is also **just,** there is no place in the Bible where we can read, *God is* **anger!** Instead, we read in 1 John 4:8, *God is Love!*

Love does not crave punishment! The very reason the cross took place was so we could avoid judgment. However, even after the cross, if we continue in our sin, what comes to us is our **own** fault; as God has made every provision for our divine pardon to take place.

> ***He who believes in Him*** *[who clings to, trusts in, relies on Him]* ***is not judged*** *[he who trusts in Him never comes up for judgment;* ***for him there is no rejection, no condemnation – he incurs no damnation];***
>
> *but he who does not believe (cleave to, rely on, trust in Him) is judged already [he has already been convicted and has already received his sentence] because he has not believed in and trusted in the name of the* ***only begotten Son*** *of God. [He is condemned for refusing to let his trust rest in Christ's name.]*
>
> *(John 3:18 AMP)*

Blood Stands Between Us And Judgement

It's impossible to be condemned if you are **in** Christ – because **Christ cannot condemn Himself!**

Grace and Freedom

*[All] **are justified** and made upright and in right standing with God, **freely** and gratuitously **by His grace** (His unmerited favor and mercy), through the redemption which is [provided] in Christ Jesus, Whom God put forward [before the eyes of all] **as a mercy seat** and propitiation by His **Blood** [the cleansing and life-giving sacrifice of atonement and reconciliation, to be received] through faith.*

*This was to show God's righteousness, because in His divine forbearance He had **passed over and ignored former sins without punishment.***

(Romans 3:24-25 AMP)

The free gift of God's grace was expressed through Jesus Christ to us, whereby we can be put right with God. Salvation is a free gift from God. Now we are **free** from sin. Satan has no more hold on us. As long as we are **in Christ,** we remain free from the **law of sin and death.**

Ongoing Liberty

Galatians 2:4 says that some will try and make us slaves once more, whilst hating our freedom in Christ. The freedom we enjoy is that we literally do not have to do **anything** to make ourselves righteous before God! Jesus has already achieved that for us. Now we can live free in His righteousness and perform the works of our God.

The old legalistic crowd tried to impose their legalism back upon the new converts of the early church, insisting that they be circumcised. But Jesus fulfilled every requirement of the law – exhausting it! Now, because of His grace *(undeserved favor)*, we no longer have to live oppressed underneath the weight of the law.

We must enjoy our liberty in Christ – for which He paid a **high price** – and not continually contend with or permit our faith to be confined by the legalism of others: man-made rules, regulations and bondage.

We are not bound – we are free indeed! *(see Matthew 15:6; Colossians 2:11-12; 13-15; Galatians 5:6; 6:15)*

Christ Did Not Set Us Free Only To Live In Bondage Again!

We have been forgiven for trying to win His approval or earn salvation in our own strength – trying to keep written codes and formulas! Legalism without grace only leaves us unfulfilled, defeated and condemned.

The way of the cross is freedom from restricting laws. It provides narrow entry to a loving relationship with the Father. **The work of the cross successfully disarmed our enemies;** we are free from wicked forces and powers of darkness. Free to live in victory; not defeat!

You were dead in trespasses and in the uncircumcision of your flesh (your sensuality, your sinful carnal nature), [God] brought to life together with [Christ], having [freely] forgiven us all our transgressions, having cancelled and blotted out and wiped away the handwriting of the note (bond) with its legal decrees and demands which was in force and stood against us (hostile to us).

This [note with its regulations, decrees, and demands] He set aside and cleared completely out of our way by nailing it to [His] cross. [God] disarmed the principalities and powers that were ranged against us and made a bold display and public example of them, in triumphing over them in Him and in it [the cross].

(Colossians 2:13-15 AMP)

❖

CHAPTER 3

United in Covenant

Fettered Together

Today, the world rejects the concept of a life-long commitment between two persons, united under a binding agreement called Marriage or more accurately **Covenant.** *It is no longer popular terminology!*

Normality in the world's eyes consists of couples outside of marriage, thinking it more correct to be called *Partners,* opposed to husband and wife. Many of these unions do not consist of opposite sexes, and do not limit themselves to include just two individuals anymore!

Yet, with the introduction of speedily arranged *same sex* marriages for the sake of ***political correctness,*** there has also been a revival of other perversions such as Bestiality, the inclusion of animals within the sex act. It has invaded our public schools and is prolific amongst teenagers, whose limit for sexual experimentation and promiscuity has no end!

Of course, the adult population is not excluded, especially the rich and famous whose notoriety has helped to turn the tide of public opinion. For the sake of *trend* they have abandoned all previous concepts of right and wrong and have dismissed morals and family values as *Old School Fundamentalism!*

This fast erosion of biblical family values is detrimental to society, as we all know that our future depends upon the continuation of the Family!

Then there are the high divorce rates for those who at least managed to commit for a season. All other premarital relations, whether bisexual or homosexual, have little if no intention of life-long commitment and are notoriously known for their duplicity of partners.

The Bible even refers to their fierce sexual appetites. Nevertheless, whatever you believe, a lifestyle of multiple partners, by any standard, is not a strong indicator of the intention of a long-term commitment. Mere courtship of pleasure, without commitment, is selfish gain and perverts the very concept of God's view of **covenant.**

Fear of commitment has caused us to lose the true meaning of covenant making. Because of this lack of understanding, we fail to recognize what we have available to us through our Covenant relationship with God.

History reveals that covenant making was the highest form of mutual commitment and union that any two individuals could make. The actual biblical meaning of Covenant is to *fetter together.* Expressly this meant that once a covenant had been made between two people, it bound them together for life, signifying to all that those two lives had become **one.**

This privilege of covenant through relationship is very special in that it is based on voluntary agreement and not force. It is binding unto death, wherein everything one owned became the joint property of the one you entered into covenant with, and vice versa.

Then, because of the **blood** involved, it became **unbreakable,** making it a lifelong commitment *broken by death alone.*

But the emphasis is on the fact that this kind of covenant could never be forced upon either party – it could only ever be entered into by volition. It was an everlasting, unchangeable and yet completely deliberate agreement.

In ancient times, participants even used to pass a sword between themselves which signified their union to any potential enemy wanting to attack. *You attack one – you attack both.* The significance of the sword was to each other, *my arms are as your arms, my weapons as your weapons.*

Yet another ceremony consisted of sandal passing from one to the other, symbolizing each other's commitment to travel as far as it might take to stand faithful at the side of their companion. Still another ritual consisted of sacrificing an animal to God, by cutting the animal in half and then proceeding to walk through the middle of it.

Walking through the sacrifice symbolized each partner's commitment to the other and that they had become half of a *new person* born of their oath.

I can also point out here that because a covenant commitment was so binding – not only including two individuals but very often also their descendants and entire families – **these lifelong pledges were extremely serious and were never entered into lightly or with much haste.**

Whether these covenant unions were entered into between friends, spouses, or man and God – no greater expression of their commitment existed. Covenant making was the deepest, highest and most enduring commitment existing between two living souls.

Covenants of the Bible

The Bible is split along Covenant lines – The Old Covenant and the New – which is more correct than saying the Old and New Testaments. During various times of biblical history we can see that seven major covenants were initiated. Six of them God made with the following: *Noah, Abraham, Isaac, Jacob, Moses, and David* (of the Old Testament) who were all partners with God in covenant.

Then, last but by no means the least, *the greatest covenant of all times:* the seventh covenant, which was made between the Father and His Son (the New Testament).

Let me stress here that the covenant was made between **the Father and the Son.** Many believers think that they have made a covenant with God when they get born again. This is only due to the lack of depth in their understanding and the little that is understood about covenant on a whole in our generation.

Covenant as a word has been largely watered down and is so far removed from its true meaning that it's little wonder that much of it is misunderstood in the Church today.

Although we are saved by Grace and not by our intellect, it is still important to come to some understanding about these things. To understand the meaning of covenant is to know our God better and the kind of relationship we have with Him. He is a Covenant making and keeping God and we are His covenant Partners – only in Christ and through Christ Jesus.

The reality, however, is that we have never cut a covenant with God and will never be required to, as there is no longer any necessity. The covenant was made or cut between the Father and the Son, an agreement to affect all humanity. It was cut on our behalf, and we enter into it first by grace and then by faith.

- Firstly *grace* because He chose to redeem us through the cutting of a covenant, without us having to do anything at all in order to win His favor.

- Secondly by *faith,* because it requires an *individual* decision to enter into that covenant and become **a covenant Partner with God.** Even more than a partner, we become **His Child** ...*whereby we cry Abba Father! (Romans 8:15)* As we stepped into Christ, we stepped **into Covenant with God** – but we didn't make the covenant – they did!

Seven Sprinklings / Seven Covenants

If we examine some of the covenants of the Bible, it will help us to understand the nature of our covenant making God, whose relationship with men was always along covenant lines.

1. The Covenant with Noah:

Genesis 6:5 reveals that the world had become so exceedingly wicked that only one man, named Noah, had found favor with God. Noah then became God's partner in a covenant that would succeed in preserving the human race.

> *I will establish My covenant (promise, pledge) with you, and you shall come into the ark – you and your sons and your wife and your sons' wives with you.*
> *(Genesis 6:18 AMP)*

Consider that, even before the flood, despite the violence and perversion that existed around Noah at that time, God was still able to preserve the righteousness of His servant.

And God commissioned him to build the ark, giving him all the blue prints necessary to build successfully according to God's invention and not Noah's humanistic mind. An invention that was able to protect God's *covenant partner* and his loved ones from the world's greatest ever catastrophe.

Contrary to how it might be taught in Sunday School, Noah never had to go and search endlessly to find the animals required to enter the ark. God brought them to Noah and after they had entered the ark, the Bible states that God closed them in. *It was God who shut the door behind them!*

Far more than just protection for Noah and his family, *the ark was the expression of a covenant* made between him and God.

Noah's name means *rest,* and it was never recorded that Noah ever questioned God. He obediently followed His every command and instruction. He rested from striving and just simply obeyed God. There is rest in obedience and there is rest in covenant relationship. You can rest secure, even in the struggle, when God is in it.

God's plan for your life is fail-proof, so when you are in covenant with God you can rest in faith and know that the outcome will be as He determined it.

When we are in covenant with God, we are supplied with great power! Alone we can achieve certain things, by sheer cleverness and resourcefulness, but being in a covenant with God provides us with much more than we are.

Whatever we try to achieve on our own merits alone – no matter how well – we are profoundly limited. Connected with the *Highest,* however, provides us with infinite resources otherwise not available to us.

It's the covenant that supplies us with all that God is. Without the covenants that were made in the Bible –

the covenant made by the **Blood** of Christ as well as those preceding – we would not be in the position that we are in today.

Each of the seven major covenants benefits every one of us; in fact, every covenant ever made between God and man has brought its benefits to humanity in one way or another. And by these covenants we have been made partakers of what was promised to them as we are descendants and heirs of all that was promised; because it climaxed and finished in Christ Jesus.

The success of a covenant does not depend so heavily upon man. In fact, the ultimate initiative is that through the success of the covenant, displaying to all creation His awesome power, God is glorified *by man.*

2. The Covenant with Abraham:

Now let's take a look at the covenant made between God and His covenant partner Abraham. Several very striking events took place during the time that God entered into covenant with Abraham, for example, the name-changing that occurred. Abram became *Abraham (a prince of God) (Genesis 17:5)* and Sarai became *Sarah (princess of God) (Genesis 17:15).*

Effectively God lifted Abraham and his wife Sarah into the royal family before cutting covenant with them!

It has been said that the most marvellous document in existence is the Abrahamic Covenant, because it is the very basis of Judaism and Christianity, and Genesis 17 reveals that circumcision sealed it. This bound Abraham and all his descendants by indissoluble ties to Jehovah and it bound Jehovah to Abraham and his descendants by the very same token.

Abraham Bound to God
God Bound to Abraham

3. The Cutting of the Covenant:

Yahweh, *God Almighty of divine power, meaning He Who IS, thus declaring His divine Self-existence,* appeared to Abram when he was 99 years old and said to him:

> *...walk and live habitually before Me and be perfect (blameless, wholehearted, complete). And I will make My covenant (solemn pledge) between Me and you and will multiply you exceedingly.*
>
> *(Genesis 17:1-2 AMP)*

And while Abram was upon his face the Lord continued:

> *As for Me, behold, My covenant (solemn pledge) is with you, and you shall be the father of many nations. **Nor shall your name any longer be Abram** [high, exalted father]; **but your name shall be Abraham** [father of a multitude], for I have made you the father of many nations.*
>
> *(Genesis 17:4-5 AMP)*

In chapter 15:6, God made a promise to Abram and it says that *Abram **believed** the Lord, and he credited it to him as righteousness.* This word *believe* here means that Abram made an ***unqualified committal*** of all that he was to God.

E.W. Kenyon says of this Hebrew word for believe that it not only means *loving trust,* but it also means *give yourself wholly up / to be part of Himself / go right into him / the unqualified committal.*

It all amounts to the fact that Abraham gave himself over to God in an act of sheer and ***utter abandonment of self.*** And as E.W. Kenyon says: "On the ground of that, God said, *'Take for me,'* that is, as God's substitute, *'an animal and slay it.'* Abraham did it.

Then God said: *'My substitute has been slain, and I want you to circumcise yourself,'* so that his **blood** would mingle with the **blood** of God's substitute.

When that was done, God and Abraham had entered the Covenant. It meant that all Abraham had or ever would have, was laid on the altar. It meant that God must sustain and protect Abraham to the very limit.

When God cut the Covenant with Abraham, the Nation of Israel came into being as a Covenant People because of this Covenant. This Covenant was limited to Israel, the children of Abraham, and had behind it the Promise and the Oath of God *(Genesis 22:16-18).*

The seal of the Covenant was circumcision. Every male child at eight days of age was circumcised, and the circumcision was the entrance into the Abrahamic Covenant. When that child was circumcised, he entered into the Covenant, and became an inheritor of everything connected with that Covenant.

If the child's father or mother should die, another Israelite is under obligation to care for the child, or if the husband should die, to care for the widow. It is the Law of the Covenant. All things are laid upon the altar of this Covenant.

The Ultimate Commitment

Even if keeping the Covenant with a Blood Brother meant the death or loss of wife, or of first born, or the destruction of his property, or of his own life, **all,** everything was laid upon the altar.

4. Covenant Obligations:

Genesis 17:13 says, *My Covenant in your flesh is to be an everlasting covenant.* Every male child at eight days of age was circumcised. This mark on their bodies was the seal of their place in the Covenant, and as long as Israel kept this Covenant that was renewed in Moses, **there weren't enemies enough in the whole world to conquer one little village.**

When God led Israel out of Egypt, by Moses, they had no law and no priesthood. Then God gave the Ten Commandments, the priesthood, the Atonement, the sacrifices, the offerings and the laws that govern the sacrifices and the offerings, the scape-goat, and the worship. All these belonged to the Covenant.

The Covenant did not belong to the Ten Commandments as modernists put it, but the Covenant was the reason for the Law. It was called the Law of the Covenant. Israel were the people of the Covenant.

5. Atonement Defined:

Read Exodus and Leviticus carefully, noting when the word *atonement* first occurs, when the Law was given, and when the priesthood was set apart. Study Leviticus 16 and 17 carefully. Note what the **blood** meant and the significance of the word *atonement*.

The word *Atonement* means to *cover*. It is not a New Testament word; it does not appear in the New Testament Greek. Why? Because the **Blood** of Jesus Christ cleanses, instead of merely covering. The first covenant did not take away sin, it merely covered it. It did not give Eternal Life or the New Birth; it only gave a promise of it" (Kenyon 15-18, 32).

6. The Covenant with Moses:

God also made covenant with Moses on Mount Sinai, but it was not an absolute warranty of divine sustenance; it was a pledge based upon national obedience to God's laws, the Ten Commandments.

The Lord's support and empowerment of His people, Israel, was conditional. It was not automatic, but *conditioned against their obedience.*

Israel put the commandments into the Ark, which preceded them into battle. God was their greatest ally and their power source was the Covenant itself. *Israel's power laid in its Covenant with God.* The whole nation inherited the promise because the Ark caused the waters to separate as they crossed the Jordan.

7. The New Covenant:

Obedience to, and trust in the Covenant conditions and the faithfulness of God, are fundamental basic elements for anyone holding a Covenant position with God as His *Covenant Partner.*

All else concerning the Covenant belongs to Him, the initiator of the whole process, which perfectly serves His divine purpose.

Israel, God's own elect people, the whole nation of them, were a Covenant People. We as Christians need to identify ourselves also as a Covenant People. Christianity is fuelled with no other power than that which flows out of this eternal Covenant we hold with God.

Redemption and reconciliation afforded us this awesome privilege of relating with God, giving us the right of Covenant Relationship. However, it only exists because of Christ's great sacrifice, His **Blood.**

The **Blood Covenant** made between the Father and the Son *(God who became Man)* is the ultimate of all Covenants, fulfilling all other Covenants. He is a Covenant making and a Covenant keeping God.

Our Covenant Making And Keeping God

It was illegal to send a perfect, sinless man to hell, but God allowed it, in Christ, thereby enabling Him to redeem all mankind and pardon their sin.

God the Father and God the Son had a divine agreement that the sin of the world would be transferred to the cross; that Christ would pay **all** of sin's debt; and that He could legally pardon **everyone** who came to the Father through Him.

Now **anyone** approaching God for forgiveness can receive it in full, thanks to the total surrender of Him, who was *infinite* presented in *finite form* (*flesh and* **Blood**) upon the cross.

Jesus kept the agreement made with His Father and never diverted once. He was faithful to the Father's cause – the terms and conditions of the Covenant with His Father were fully obeyed. Nothing missing or left undone, which is why Jesus declared from the cross, **it is finished** – completed in full!

And because of its completion, it was established for eternity, never to be undone.

The accuser of the brethren continually seeks to condemn us for our sins, but we must remember to declare the righteous **Blood** of our faithful Savior.

Salvation was not secured upon any other foundation than that of the Covenant (*agreement*) made between Jesus and His Father. However, Satan still tries to convince us daily that salvation is based upon our efforts, when there is nothing any of us could ever have achieved to save us from our sin.

Jesus was the only hope we had – there was no Plan B in store! **It was Jesus' success or our failure.** Praise God, He succeeded, and that success stands forever.

Stand On The Blood Covenant And Waver Not

We are saved and forgiven because Christ succeeded and **His Blood sealed it for eternity.** Now the destroyer has to *Passover.* So, when the accuser does what the accuser is meant to do – accuse us – we need to do what we are meant to do – stand on the **Blood Covenant,** and waver not!

Consider this: Jesus did not covenant with a mere human being, weakened by the flesh, unfaithful and radically limited. No. In actual fact, *infinity* covenanted with *infinity!* **God made covenant with God!**

> *And if we are [His] children, then we are [His] heirs also:* ***heirs of God*** *and* ***fellow heirs with Christ*** *[sharing His inheritance with Him].*
>
> *(Romans 8:17 AMP)*

We need to find out what Christ is enjoying, and make sure that we too are enjoying the same *(our inheritance).* If we are not enjoying those same privileges, then it indicates that we are not **in** Christ and are still bound to the things of this world.

For example, we ought to be enjoying safety, security, protection, prosperity, health, joy and fulfillment, for this is our Covenant right – sealed in the **Blood** of Christ. Jesus came that we should have life and have it more abundantly. This is not a flesh life, but a fulfilled life!

God Is On Our Side

Back to Back We Stand

Consider the family of Noah, who enjoyed safety, security and protection **only** because of the covenant made between God and Noah. Then there was Abraham, who we also looked at in some depth previously, whose descendants would not still be enjoying all the rights and privileges they obtained, if it were not for the Covenant made between Abraham and God.

Abraham kept the terms of the Covenant with God, and gained all that was promised – a covenant established forever. Noah kept and was faithful and obedient to all the terms and conditions of the

Covenant made between him and God, thereby gaining all the promises laid out. It was a Covenant established forever. In fact, every single common **rainbow** still serves as a reminder to every generation of the Covenant made between Noah and his God.

Again, all this amounts to and can be gathered up into the fact that God is a *Covenant Keeping God.* And when we consider all other Covenants, this only helps to reinforce our understanding of the unique and ultimate *Covenant!*

Our confidence is boosted to know that every promise and victory secured through the **Blood Covenant** of Christ and the Father, benefits humanity yesterday, today, and forever, throughout endless time!

Willingly He Came
From As Far As Eternity
To Be At Our Side

Francis Frangipane states in his book *The Place of Immunity* that, because of Jesus, the sandal of divine commitment – **God's willingness to come from as far as eternity to be at our side** – is given to us.

The sword has been passed between us – God and His covenant partners are united against evil. Our enemies of sickness, poverty and fear are His enemies. His enemies of sin and Satan are our adversaries as well. **God and man are back to back against our common foes.**

God And Man Pass Through The Halves

The covenant animal of sacrifice is not a bull or a goat, it is a Lamb. God and man pass through the *halves* of Christ. **We unite with God through Christ's humanity; God unites with us through Christ's divinity.** In Jesus, God and man become one in covenant power (Frangipane 64).

Conclusion

Covenant is an agreement between two or more persons involving five main elements:

- Prophecy
- The parties present
- Conditions present
- Results
- Security

1. Prophecy:

For example, the predicting throughout Scripture concerning the two advents of Christ: His First and Second Coming, i.e. the Abrahamic and Davidic covenants.

2. The Parties Present:

The covenant may be between individual men; between nations, or between God and man. For example, God the Father and the Son were the chief originating parties of the *Covenant of Redemption;* Christ being the Mediator of this covenant, while God and individual men, including Israel, were its efficacious partners.

The Father and the Son were the chief parties of the Covenant of Grace. God the Father covenanted with Christ to save, by grace, those who believe in the Son and His substitutionary death.

This covenant became the foundation of Romans 4 and Hebrews 11, the two main passages concerning justification by faith in the New Testament.

In the Old Testament individuals entered into this covenant through their saving faith in and acceptance of the type of Christ in the Old Testament and in the New Testament individuals enter by the same faith, with acceptance of the antitype, even Jesus Christ Himself.

3. Conditions Present:

Covenants are either **unilateral** *(one-sided)* or **bilateral** *(two-sided)*. All human covenants are bilateral, and covenants between God and man are mainly unilateral.

Examples of unilateral covenants between God and man are *the Abrahamic Covenant, the Davidic Covenant* and *the **New Covenant.*** One example of a bilateral covenant between God and man was the Mosaic covenant.

Yet we must see, without any confusion, that even the essentially unilateral covenants have a bilateral aspect insofar as their application has regard to individual men. We can also see that the seal, sign or token of one, having accepted the covenant relationship by an act of individual faith, is a step of obedience.

Even in the Abrahamic covenant, the sign of which was circumcision *(Genesis 17:10-11)*, the sign was stated as a part of individual application of the covenant. Any attempt to separate the unilateral element of the Abrahamic covenant from its individual application becomes artificial, and the acknowledgement therefore of both factors – unilateral and bilateral – in such a covenant, becomes necessary.

- **Unilateral** *(one-sided, single, and partial)*

  It is unconditional, based upon God's Sovereignty, i.e. His sovereign Grace. It is an unconditional covenant because it is complete, absolute, and pure. It is predictable because it is entirely dependent upon no other response than that of sovereign decision – **Grace!** *(New Testament)*

- **Bilateral** *(shared, collective, mutual, joint and co-operative)*

  It is conditional, based upon the necessity of an individual and personal response of acceptance by faith. A conditional covenant is lesser and secondary because it is dependent, subordinate and contingent. It is unpredictable because it depends upon a response or upon the willingness thereof.

In like manner, water baptism is the sign or seal of one's membership in the new covenant community.

Examination shows that *unilateral* elements in a covenant are prophetic, and thereby immutable; whereas the *bilateral* elements are soteriological *(doctrine of salvation),* and therefore conditional to the extent that they are dependent upon personal acceptation by faith, with motivation coming through God's sovereign grace.

4. Results:

Dependent upon saving faith, these can either be promises of blessing when the covenant is kept, or warnings of punishment when the covenant is broken, or both.

Abraham was promised a seed, land, fame, posterity – all prophetic and certain – while at the same time conditional because the believing participant was required to be circumcised as a seal of his faith. Those who refused to be circumcised broke the covenant *(Genesis 17:14).*

As Christians we are circumcised by the ...*circumcision of Christ* *(Colossians 2:11).*

5. Security:

Usually the guarantee given was either by oath or by the slaying of an animal, in order to seal the covenant. At other times a gift was given or a sign set up *(Genesis 21:30; 31:52).*

But because God can swear by nothing greater than Himself, He confirmed His covenants by swearing by Himself *(Deuteronomy 29:12; Hebrews 6:13-14)* or swearing by His providential control of the world *(Jeremiah 31:35; 33:20)* (Wycliffe Bible Encyclopedia 386).

What is the New Covenant Specifically?

The New Covenant is a covenant of **Redemption and Grace** – *God's plan through Jesus Christ to redeem His elect (Psalm 40:6-8; Hebrews 10:5-14)* and it was dedicated by the **Blood** of Christ *(Hebrews 9:13-15)*.

Christ died because He was charged with making the New Covenant with man. Since the victims *(man)* involved were under the penalty of death for their sins, and since the covenant had to do with the redemption of these victims by the death of a substitute, it was necessary for the one making the covenant to die in order to redeem them and free them from death *(Hebrews 9:16)*.

Such a covenant could only be in force after the victim was dead and the covenant ratified *(legalized, validated)* by such a death *(verse 17)*.

Covenant Means:

- League
- Confederacy *(alliance, coalition)*
- To fetter together
- To make

- To cut
- To set, put, and arrange together
- A pact
- *A last will and testament*
- To establish, appoint a compact

And all involves various transactions between parties, where one voluntarily binds oneself to fulfil the certain conditions required and likewise receives the certain advantages promised.

Covenant is central throughout the whole Bible and reveals Gods ultimate covenant purpose: to reconcile man to Himself; where man can enjoy a life of unbroken fellowship with Him, made possible through the redemption that is available in Christ Jesus.

❖

CHAPTER 4

The Seven-Fold Sprinkling

The Levitical Priesthood

During the time of the Exodus, when God used Moses to lead His people out of Egypt, there was no priesthood, no Law and no Ten Commandments. Before the Law existed, there was no need for priests of Levitical order because there were no boundaries that could reveal personal right and wrong!

However, with the existence of the Law came the knowledge of sin, which created the need for the people to have someone who could stand for them, in order that their sins could be covered. And it was for this very reason that God ordained the Levitical Priesthood.

*Before the law was given, sin was in the world. But **sin is not taken into account when there is no law.** Nevertheless, death reigned from the time of Adam to the time of Moses, even over those who did not sin by breaking a command, as did Adam, who was a pattern of the one to come.*

(Romans 5:13-14)

What Purpose did the Law Have?

What we call the Old *Covenant* was made up of the Ten Commandments, the priesthood, the atonement, the sacrifices and all the laws that they had to govern their offerings and worship.

The *Covenant* did not belong to the Law *(Ten Commandments)*, but instead was the reason for the Law, which is why it was called the *Law of the Covenant.* In other words, the Covenant did not exist for the Law – the Law existed for the Covenant. And the Israelites were the *People of the Covenant.*

The Law was added to the Covenant because of **sin.**

*What, then, was the purpose of the law? **It was added because of transgressions** until the Seed to whom the promise referred had come.*

(Galatians 3:19)

*We know that the law is good if one uses it properly. We also know that **law is made** not **for the** righteous but for lawbreakers and rebels, the **ungodly and sinful, the unholy and irreligious;***

for those who kill their fathers and mothers, for murderers, for adulterers and perverts, for slave traders and liars and perjurers – and for whatever else is contrary to the sound doctrine...

(1 Timothy 1:8-10)

Access to the Holy Place:

Bill Basansky, in his book *Life and Power of the Blood Covenant* says on page 34: "The Levitical priesthood came into being as a result of the law. In the law of Israel, *a High Priest could not enter the Holy of Holies unless his heart was pure.* His body had to be washed with water and dressed in garments ordained by God.

Only Purity Of Heart
Can Stand Before True Holiness

No person could touch the High Priest before he entered the Holy of Holies *(where God the Father was)* to offer a **blood** sacrifice for his sins, as well as the sins of his family, the people and the nation of Israel.

First, he would offer a bullock as atonement for *his* sins and the sins of *his* house *(Leviticus 16:11)*. Then he would put incense upon the fire before the Lord so a cloud of incense would cover the *mercy seat;* otherwise it meant his *death!* *(Leviticus 16:13; Exodus 25:21-22)*

(Note: the mercy seat was placed on top of the Ark of the Covenant between the two cherubim, in the Holy of Holies and is where God's presence was revealed and His voice was heard; giving instructions to His people.)

The cloud created by the burning incense obscured any possibility of the High Priest seeing God's presence, which in turn prevented his death! **No man could see God and live.**

Blood upon the Mercy Seat:

He was also required to sprinkle **blood** across the mercy seat and before the mercy seat **seven times** *(Leviticus 16:14).* The result of the **blood** sprinkling caused the *Shekinah Glory* of God *(that is, God Himself)* to be manifested in the Holy of Holies; speaking to the High Priest from between the two cherubim that overshadowed the mercy seat *(Hebrews 9:1-12)*" (Basansky 34).

Notice how God appeared to the High Priest, not just because the Priest had faith in the **blood,** but because he **activated the blood.**

The Blood Must Be Activated

Office of the High Priest:

Bill Basansky states on this subject: "These were the priests of the Aaronic family. The only claim to this office was sonship. There were many priests, and their work was to minister in holy matters.

Aaron was the first High Priest and after him only one High Priest held office at any one time. Yet, according to the historian Josephus, there were more than eighty men officiating in this capacity between Aaron, the first priest, and Christ. The only reason for the change of one priest to another was death.

The Aaronic priesthood continued with its lamb sacrifices until the death of Christ in the days of Caiaphas, the High Priest. Then it ended, for Christ, the perfect Lamb of God had died once and for all, passed within the veil and sat down at the right hand of Majesty on High.

Thus, becoming our **Great High Priest,** He took upon Himself the ministry of intercession – not only for the firstborn *(as under the law)* – but He obligated Himself to all who would believe and follow Him *(Mark 16:15-20; John 3:16; Romans 10:9-10; Hebrews 8:1)"* (Basansky 34).

Sprinkling of the Precious Blood:

God foretold the shedding of the **Blood** of Jesus through the Old Testament. For example, in Leviticus chapter 16, God foretold that there would be a **seven-fold sprinkling** of the precious **Blood** of Jesus.

So we need to go through the successive seven-fold steps of the sprinkling of the **Blood** of Jesus as recorded in the Gospels.

First of all, in the Garden of Gethsemane as He prayed in agony, His sweat fell down *like great drops of **blood*** on the ground. Then, when they took Him to the house of the High Priest and began to abuse Him, they struck Him across the face with rods and brought out the **Blood.**

At some point of their mistreatment of Him they began to pull out the hair of His beard in tufts and of course the **Blood** came out. Then He was handed over by Pontius Pilot to be scourged.

Now a Roman scourge was a whip with many thongs in which were embedded pieces of bone and metal. And so, as the thongs fell across a man's back, they literally tore open the flesh.

Then in mockery, because He claimed to be a King, they planted a crown of thorns upon His head. *(The same type of thorns can still be seen if you go to Israel today – they are long, hard and very sharp.)* They pressed those thorns down into His scalp, causing the **Blood** to well up and run down into His face and body.

Isaiah prophetically predicted this:

> *Just as there were many who were appalled at him – his appearance **was so disfigured beyond that of any man and his form marred beyond human likeness –** so will he sprinkle many nations, and kings will shut their mouths because of him.*
>
> *(Isaiah 52:14-15)*

He predicted that Jesus' visage was so marred that He lost even the appearance of a human being! Then they nailed Him to the cross and put nails through His hands and His feet. And finally, after He was dead, a soldier thrust a spear through His side in the area of the heart; **Blood** and water gushed out.

This completes the **seven-fold sprinkling** predicted by the Ceremony of the *Day of Atonement:*

1. His sweat like great drops of **blood.**

2. The beating with rods at the house of the High Priest

3. The beard-pulling

4. The scourging

5. The painful crown of thorns

6. The nailing to the cross

7. The final thrust of a soldier's spear into His side

In Leviticus 17:11 AMP it says:

> For **the life** (the animal soul) **is in the blood,** and I have given it for you upon the altar to make atonement for your souls; for **it is the Blood that makes atonement, by reason of the life** [which it represents].

This is yet another amazing prophecy of the Old Testament: not just a regulation of whether or not an Israelite should eat food with or without **blood,** but a prediction of the **Cross!**

The life is in the Blood and I have given it to you upon the altar of Calvary to make atonement for your souls. And then, in Isaiah 53:12 in the great prophetic picture of the atonement, Isaiah says that He *...poured out his soul unto death.*

How did He do that? By His **Blood.** The soul is in the **Blood** and Jesus poured out His soul as a *Sin Offering* for the whole human race. His soul took the place of our souls and became the *final* sin offering.

> He **poured out his soul** unto death, and he was numbered with the transgressors; and he bore the sin of many, and made intercession for the transgressors.
>
> *(Isaiah 53:12 NKJ)*

71

Why Seven?

For further study and for your own personal reference, this is a brief look at the significance of the number seven throughout the Scriptures:

- **Seven** Sprinklings
- **Seven** major Covenants
- The Passover was a **seven**-day feast
- **Seven** times round Jericho
- And so forth. Why continually **seven?**

Following below, Kevin J. Conner briefly maps out *The Seven Times* issue for us as seen in his manual *The Feasts of Israel.*

The Seven Times Sprinkling of Blood:

"The sprinkling of the **Blood** 7 times on the Mercy Seat was prophetic of the perfect atonement that Christ would bring to His people." Kevin J. Conner also believes that, "Throughout the Scripture, the theme of *The Seven Times* becomes prophetic of the end of the age and that which finds its ultimate in the seventh day of the Lord, the Kingdom Age" *(Leviticus 16:14).*

Seven: Fullness, Perfection And The Close Of The Age

"The following are some of the examples of these *Seven Times* prophecies, **the number seven speaking of fullness,**

perfection and the close of the present age as ushered in by Christ's coming."

1. Jacob bowed down to Esau **seven times** *(Genesis 33:3)*

2. **Blood** was sprinkled **seven times** *(Leviticus 4:6; 8:11; 14:7; 16:14-17)*

3. Israel was to be punished **seven times** for her sins *(Leviticus 26:18,21,24,28)*

4. The walls of Jericho were compassed about **seven times** before its collapse *(Joshua 6:4-15)*

5. Elijah prayed and then after **seven times** great rain fell *(1 Kings 18:43)*

6. The furnace of persecution was heated **seven times** when the Hebrew believers were cast in and preserved *(Daniel 3:19)*

7. Naaman immersed himself **seven times** before his healing took place *(2 Kings 5:10)*

8. Oil was sprinkled **seven times** in the cleansing of the leper *(Leviticus 14:16-18)*

9. Forgiveness is to be beyond **seven times** *(Matthew 18:21-22)*

Mr Conner goes on to say, "Thus the **Seven Times** sprinkling of **blood** became symbolic and prophetic of the perfections that the **Blood** of Jesus will bring to His church in the end-times and at His coming.

In the Passover Feast the **blood** was sprinkled upon the door. In the Pentecost Feast the blood was sprinkled on the people and the Covenant Book. In tabernacles the blood was sprinkled seven times on the Mercy Seat.

The Day of Atonement in the church will be the fullest manifestation of the power of the **Blood** of Jesus. It will bring the church to perfection, making an end of all sin, all iniquity, all transgressions and all sins of ignorance and all uncleanness" (Conner 57).

❖

CHAPTER 5

Christ is the True Passover

The Blood of the Lamb

Now, before we go any further, I want to deal with something extremely practical, because what I have described to you about the Blood is true and wonderful, but it doesn't mean *that you know how* to make it real and personal in your own life and experience.

So, I want to teach you how to *appropriate (take possession of, take to oneself)* **the Blood of Jesus** and how to get the full effects of the **Blood** of Jesus working in your life.

By way of introduction, we'll first take a look at Revelation 12:11. This speaks about what I believe to be a great end-time conflict that lays ahead, at the close of this present age. A conflict in which heaven and earth are involved, including the angels of God; Satan and his angels; and the Church – believers on earth.

Thank God that the victory goes to God and to His people!

> *They have overcome (conquered) him by means of the **Blood** of the Lamb and by the **utterance** of their testimony, for they did not love and cling to life even when faced with death [holding their lives cheap till they had to die for their witnessing].*
>
> *(Revelation 12:11 AMP)*

This passage describes how the people of God on earth – believers – played their part in obtaining that victory. It's a statement made by the angels, but it concerns believers on earth.

Direct Conflict

"They" refers to believers in Jesus Christ and *"him"* to Satan. This is very important to recognize because right here it shows very clearly that there can be **direct conflict** between Satan and us – there is no one else in between: ***They** overcame **him...***

Then it reveals just *how* they overcame him: *"...by means of the **Blood** of the Lamb and by the **utterance** of their testimony."* Defining their character with *"...they did not love and cling to life even when faced with death."*

In a word, they were **committed.** Totally committed, and that's the only type of Christian that frightens Satan – radically committed, and not possessed with self-preservation!

Radically Committed

"...they did not love and cling to life even when faced with death." What does that actually mean? For them it meant that staying alive was not their primary objective! Priority number one, whether it meant they stayed alive or not, was to be faithful to the Lord and to do His will.

We talk about being soldiers in the Lord's army, but I think a lot of us have a very vague and rather sentimental idea of what it is to be a soldier. For example, when people join the army, they do not receive a nice little certificate from their Commanding Officer ensuring them that they will never have to lose their life! The opposite is the case.

No soldier has ever joined the army on the condition that he will never be killed! One of the commitments that a soldier has to make when he joins the army is that it *may* indeed cost him his life – no guarantees!

Every soldier has to come to terms with that fact, and it's just the same with the Lord's army. We have **no** guarantees that we will not have to lay down our lives; rather we are commissioned to take up our cross daily!

The type of Christian that Satan fears is the one who fears not to lay down his life; knowing that *he who tries to save his life will lose it and he who loses it will save it! (Matthew 10:39; Luke 17:33)* Besides, as life on earth is relatively short, no temporal relief can be compared to the *eternal weight of Glory to be revealed in us (see Acts 7:55).*

Enlightened Self-Interest

I believe it is *enlightened self-interest* to have a proper sense of values. What can be more important? I believe that we should say, *For me the most important thing in life is to do the will of God.*

There's a wonderful saying in 1 John 2:17 AMP which says, *The world passes away and disappears, and with it the forbidden cravings (the passionate desires, the lust) of it;* **but he who does the will of God and carries out His purposes in his life abides** *(remains)* **forever.**

When we unite our will with the will of God in total commitment, we become just as unsinkable and unshakable as the very Will of God itself! When we identify ourselves with the will of God, whether we live or die carrying it out, ultimately we cannot be defeated. In Christ we are *more than* conquerors!

Unsinkable and Unshakable

Now, let's consider what it really means to overcome Satan...*by means of the* **Blood** *of the Lamb and by the* **Word of our testimony.**

Derek Prince states on the subject, **"We overcome Satan, when we testify personally to what the Word of God says the Blood of Jesus does for us."**

We Must Testify
What The Blood Does For Us

Firstly, I want to take an example from the Old Testament. We'll begin by looking at the *Passover Ceremonies* recorded in Exodus chapter 12, where we must remember that during the Passover, God used the sacrifice of a Passover lamb to provide total protection for all the people of Israel. However, they had to do certain practical things with the Lamb and with its **blood** to ensure that protection.

The True Passover:

1 Corinthians 5:7 KJV says, ...***Christ, our Passover is sacrificed for us...*** meaning that the Old Testament Passover was just a preview of what was to be accomplished by the sacrificial death of Jesus upon the cross. ***Christ is the true Passover*** – it is **His Blood** that finally assures us of eternal redemption.

However, the way that Israel was instructed to apply the **blood** of the lamb is a wonderful pattern for us. This ordinance of the Passover also illustrates *the tremendous responsibility of being a Father,* because the only persons in Israel who could obtain safety and salvation for their people, were *the Fathers of Israel.*

Delinquent Fathers

Derek Prince said, ***"If the Fathers of Israel had been delinquent, Israel would not have been protected by the Passover."*** He went on to state, *"The greatest single social problem that faces us is **delinquent fathers.**" (Delinquent = slack, neglectful and failing in duty).* **Note: the problem of delinquency does not rest with the children but with the parents!**

"All the problems that we are concerned about: abortion, drugs, the breakup of the family, and many, many other social evils, I believe if you trace them to their source, their source is delinquent fathers."

I have pointed out the responsibilities of fathers in this context, because if the fathers had failed, Israel would never have been redeemed. **God's plan depended on the Fathers.**

*Moses summoned all the elders of Israel and said to them, "Go at once and select the animals for your families and slaughter the Passover lamb. **Take a bunch of hyssop, dip it into the Blood in the basin and put some of the Blood on the top and on both sides of the door-frame.** Not one of you shall go out the door of his house until morning.*

*When the Lord goes through the land to strike down the Egyptians, he will see the **Blood** on the top and sides of the door-frame and will **Pass Over** that doorway, and he will not permit the destroyer to enter your houses and strike you down.*

(Exodus 12:21–23)

That's why it is called the *Passover* because the Lord said that He would *pass over* the door that was protected by the **Blood** of the lamb.

Two Million Came To Dinner

This was a day when two million slaves prepared a feast for themselves, a feast for a King. Something was different, everyone was in unity and the Egyptians at this moment looked on, wondering what was amiss. Perhaps asking the question, *What on earth are those crazy Israelites up to now?*

The air was filled with a delicious smell, an aroma of two hundred and fifty thousand lambs being roasted on spits, with the Israelites praying and praising their God, the God of Abraham, Isaac and Jacob!

This must have brought a sense of confusion to the Egyptians as they asked the question, *Have they gone mad?* But it's true to say that when we participate in the eating of the lamb and rejoicing in the Lord in the face of our enemies, in the face of bondage and oppression, we too will confuse and overthrow the bondage of the devil.

> *Thou preparest a table before me* **in the presence of mine enemies:** *thou anointest my head with oil; my cup runneth over.*
>
> *(Psalm 23:5 KJV)*

When the lambs were slaughtered, the Israelites had to dip a bunch of **hyssop,** a bitter herb, symbolizing their bondage, into the **Blood,** and paint the posts and lintels of their doors. Then all the families were supposed to *walk through* the door and *eat every scrap* of the meat which they had cooked.

Did they do so with a growing, amazed realization that they were partaking in a covenant meal? Perhaps. Moses certainly knew that all that was happening was the outworking of God's covenant promise, so he may not have been as astonished as the rest of them when they **ate the lamb and found themselves healed of every affliction!**

We Walked Through The Blood
And Ate The Bread Of Repentance

They had walked through the walls of **Blood,** just as one would do in a covenant sacrifice. And now they were eating a meal and breaking unleavened bread together, the *bread of repentance,* making a statement, therefore, that they were *leaving behind sin,* as if to finalize that covenant.

Deliverance, freedom, wholeness, destiny, and the hand of God had come. And the encouraging thing from our point of view is that they had not shown mountains of faith or deep spiritual understanding in the past.

Deliverance
And The Hand Of God Had Come

All they did was **obey** God. They fed on the right food which, in a spiritual sense, was the Lamb of God, the Word of Christ Himself, even though they had no idea that this act prefigured the new **Passover,** the deliverance that would come to **all** mankind through the sacrifice of the Lamb.

Ian Andrews says, "After years of poverty and ill treatment not a single one of the two million Israelites stumbled or fainted on the way. Weak and undernourished as they must have been before the Passover meal, now they were supernaturally restored and empowered with the strength for this epic escape in the face of huge dangers and obstacles.

What a remarkable thing! What an encouragement for us to see the life and restoration available in the **Blood** of Jesus, the New Passover Lamb" (Andrews 61).

Now let's consider what they had to Do!

At a certain given moment *each father* had to choose a lamb of appropriate size for his family and sacrifice it. They had to catch its **blood** in a basin; its **blood** was very precious, **none** of it was to be spilled upon the ground. However, even though the **blood** was their means of *protection,* while still in the basin, it didn't protect anyone!

Blood Has To Be Applied

They were required to transfer the **blood** from the basin to the doors of their homes, to smear it or to sprinkle it on the doorframes, the two side-posts, but never on the threshold. **No one walks on the Blood!**

No Demon In Hell
Can Trespass The Blood

Everything – the whole destiny of Israel – depended on getting the Blood from the basin to the door – with that little bunch of hyssop!

God told them to pluck this little bunch of **hyssop** (*a bitter weed that grows everywhere in the Middle East*) and dip it into the **blood** from the basin and then sprinkle it over the door. This is striking: watch how something as common as this little bunch of **hyssop** became so vital to God's plan of salvation for an entire nation!

The same applies to our tongue: a common insignificant little thing, but what a part it plays in our salvation! (*see Romans 10:10*)

Later on we see **hyssop** playing yet another centre-stage role in the New Testament! First we saw its bitter involvement in the salvation of the Nation of Israel; only to see it again, taking part within the ultimate salvation scene of **all** mankind, which was acted out upon the cross.

What significance should we lend to this? Why does such a normally insignificant object enjoy such centre-stage prominence in the history of mankind, and on more than one occasion?

> *A vessel (bowl) full of sour wine (vinegar) was placed there, so they put a sponge soaked in the sour wine on [a stalk, reed of]* **hyssop**, *and held it to [His] mouth. When Jesus had received the sour wine, He said,* **It is finished!** *And He bowed His head and gave up His spirit.*
> *(John 19:29 AMP)*

Everything recorded in the Holy Writings is there with good purpose and intention *(see 2 Timothy 3:16)*. Therefore, **hyssop's** role, recorded forever, is highly significant and we must not rush to overlook it or underestimate its involvement.

The first time round we see **hyssop** being dipped into the **blood of the lamb.** The second time round, we see **hyssop** being dipped into vinegar/bitter wine and given **to the Lamb!**

In both instances **hyssop** has been used as a carrier or vehicle. A carrier of the **blood,** then a carrier of the bitter potion. Hyssop is bitter, and Christ tasted of that bitter cup of **sin** for all of us. Having received it for us He cried, **It is finished!**

Christ is the True Passover

The tongue is a fire. [The tongue is a] world of wickedness
set among our members, contaminating and depraving the
whole body and setting on fire the wheel of birth (the cycle
of man's nature), **being itself ignited by hell** (Gehenna).
...a restless evil, **full of deadly poison.**

(James 3:6-8 AMP)

In recognition of the fact that one of hyssop's roles is
likened to that of the tongue, its most serious connotation
lies in the fact that our tongues are able to carry, or be the
very vehicle for, either life or death! *(Proverbs 18:21; 13:2-3;
21:23; Matthew 12:37)*

Death and life are in the power of the tongue and they
who indulge in it shall eat the fruit of it [for death or life].

(Proverbs 18:21 AMP)

To summarize then, in the Old Testament **hyssop**
represented the bitter treatment of the children of Israel in
Egypt, but in the New Testament it chiefly represents our
tongues *(our confessions)*. We can **choose life or death** with
the very words of our mouths.

I call heaven and earth to record this day against you,
that I have set before you life and death, blessing
and cursing: therefore choose life, that both thou and
thy seed may live.

(Deuteronomy 30:19 KJV)

*That if thou shalt **confess with thy mouth** the Lord*
Jesus, and shalt believe in thine heart that God hath raised
him from the dead, thou shalt be saved. For with the heart

*man believeth unto righteousness; and **with the mouth confession is made unto salvation.***

(Romans 10:9-10 KJV)

Besides this mingled drink *(Matthew 27:48, John 19:29)* that Jesus was offered *(Mark 15:23)*, carried to him on **hyssop,** it was nine o'clock in the morning when they nailed Him to the cross, and He died only six hours later at three in the afternoon.

Significant to note is that this was the same time that the Passover lambs were to be slaughtered *(Matthew 27:45-50; Luke 23:44-46)* which fulfilled the 22nd prophecy of the Old Testament *(Psalm 69:21)*.

It is important to know that such a mingled drink as they offered Him was customary of that time, usually an intoxicating potion, to alleviate suffering *(Proverbs 31:6)*.

While some believe that Jesus took some of this potion, it remains clear that Jesus rejected **any relief** from the cross. His death was totally deliberate and voluntary, therefore it is safe to assume that Jesus not only chose to exhaust sin's suffering penalty, but did so while fully sober and in His right mind!

No man taketh it from me, but I lay it down of myself. I have power to lay it down, and I have power to take it again.

(John 10:17–18 KJV)

❖

CHAPTER 6

The Blood is not Sprinkled on the Disobedient

Obedience and the Blood

Once this **blood** had been sprinkled on their doors, they had to stay inside their houses. *They were not permitted beyond the Blood!* Even today, without the **Blood** covering, there is **no protection.** You can shout about it in Church, but unless you adhere to and activate the **Blood** – it does not apply to **you** or your house.

> *Peter, an apostle of Jesus Christ, to God's elect, strangers in the world, scattered throughout Pontus, Galatia, Cappadocia, Asia and Bithynia, who have been chosen according to the foreknowledge of God the Father, through*

*the sanctifying work of the Spirit, **for obedience to Jesus Christ and sprinkling by his Blood:** Grace and peace be yours in abundance.*

(1 Peter 1:1-2)

Obedience Comes Before The Sprinkling

It's important to notice that **obedience** came before sprinkling. Obedience to Jesus Christ comes first. **Blood is not sprinkled on the disobedient.**

It did not avail anybody to disobey or venture outside of his house. So, bear in mind that **although there *is* perfect protection in the Blood, it is only for those who *stay in* obedience!**

Ceremony:

Now let's return to the Passover ceremony. Remember the **blood** was in the basin, and had to be transferred to the door. There was an apprehended bunch of hyssop, which had been dipped into the **blood** and used to sprinkle that same **blood** onto the doorframes of their homes. Once applied they were safe – but only if they stayed **inside!**

Paul says that Christ is our Passover, who was sacrificed for us. In other words, Christ was slain 2000 years ago, but if you like, **the Blood is effectively still in its catching basin. Why? Because most people hear, but don't apply.**

The Blood Must Travel

We are in the same situation as Israel was in, and **we have to get the Blood from the basin to the doorframes of our lives.** Then we can be sure of protection – provided we live in obedience.

So how do we get the Blood from the basin? What will transport it? We have no **hyssop** but we have our **tongues!** To qualify our theory, see Revelation 12:11 where it clearly says, **...they overcame him by the *Blood* of the Lamb and by the *Word* of their testimony.** This is a direct reference to the fact that our **tongues** must work together in unison with the **Blood!**

We Overcome Satan When We Say What God Says About The Blood!

The Blood Transfer:

So, what is it that enables us to transfer the **Blood?** It's not enough to just say the **tongue.** The simple answer is: our **Testimony.** Our testimony and what we say about the **Blood** is how we apply it. Our confession of faith about what the **Blood** has done for us! The application of the Lamb's **Blood** still forces evil to **pass over** our lives today.

Testimony defined is very simply just *saying a few words in accordance with Scripture.* It's like the little hyssop that appeared insignificant and unimportant, but was the very tool God chose to apply the **blood,** which in turn provided *absolute* protection and salvation from destruction. It still stands today! The same yesterday, today and forever!

Meanings for the word *testimony:*

- Evidence / proof / support / verification
- Confirmation / avowal / attestation
- Demonstration / oath / confession / admission
- Oral or written statement under oath or affirmation
- Declarations / acknowledgement / corroboration
- Statements / pledge / assertion / announcement / pronouncement
- Solemn protest or confession
- The Scriptures

When we testify *(Revelation 12:2 ...by the word of their testimony)* we are literally giving evidence, affirmation and declaration to the truth – the Word of God. **Verbally** *affirming* **what God has said and done has powerful ramifications and repercussions in our lives!**

The Tongue's Influence:

Let's take another closer look at the *effects* of our words, whether serious or in jest. In fact, words are very often idle. We often hear people saying, *Oh, I didn't really mean what I said. I just said it.* That's simply because they've never really been taught the value of their words according to the Scriptures.

> ***Every idle word*** *that men shall speak, they shall give account thereof in the day of judgement.* ***For by thy words thou shalt be justified, and by thy words thou shalt be condemned.***
>
> *(Matthew 12:36-37 KJV)*

The Greek word for *idle* is *argos,* which has the following meanings *(found in the Strong's Concordance #G692):*

- inactive
- unemployed
- lazy
- useless
- barren
- idle
- slow

What a sober thought. It makes you want to straighten out your speech straight away! The reality is that in our day and age, the value of words has been absolutely depleted. Nevertheless, **words** are selling at a tremendous rate, in every form of the media.

Words are still essential, for without them life would have no meaning! Advertising would have limited effect without its most powerful vehicle – **words.** Images are meaningless without words!

In yesteryear we all understood that a man's word was his bond. But today it is just nonsense, especially in the business world. In the eyes of the world, only the written word provides proof, whereas anything unrecorded has no legal pull or weight.

Yet, Scripture states it differently. I believe the Bible indicates that **words of any kind are eternal.** They speak forth the power of death or the power of life. Words are carriers, which is why Jesus said, *...the words that I speak to you are spirit, and they are life (John 6:63 NKJ).* **Jesus knew the value and meaning of His every word.**

Nothing idle or careless would have left His lips – He was a man without sin. In Isaiah 53:9 AMP it says about Jesus, *...they assigned Him a grave with the wicked, and with a rich man in His death, although He had done no violence, **neither was any deceit in His mouth.***

So he ***never*** sinned, not even once with his mouth *(1 Peter 2:22; Matthew 27:57-60).* This sounds incredible to those who live according to the flesh and the carnal flow of this world.

Let it all hang out, is the ugly motto of this world: *speak your mind; unleash your thoughts; off-load your confusion on someone else; vomit your verbal garbage on anyone who will listen! Vent your anger; mock and curse; don't hold back – **express yourself without restraint!***

Jesus Only Ever Spoke the Word Of Faith

Whatsoever is not of faith is sin.

(Romans 14:23 KJV)

Romans 14:23 AMP says, ***...whatever does not originate and proceed from faith is sin*** *[whatever is done without a conviction of its approval by God is sinful].* That means that Jesus only ever spoke words of faith. Had any one of His words been void of faith, then sin *(deceit)* would have been found in His mouth, **but He was *without* sin.**

Hyssop and the Tongue

I want to compare our careless, idle, good-for-nothing words that are rolled around all day and every day as *idle or barren* chatter, to this small, bushy, aromatic herb from the Middle East.

What we have been duped into believing all our lives as being something insignificant, not important and of little value, *namely our spoken words and the tongue,* are in reality just like hyssop – an incredibly simple vehicle by which we obtain protection and salvation! *Just think on that for a moment!*

Our Words Must Also Be Dipped Into The Blood

Just like that little bunch of hyssop, *our words must also be dipped into the Blood and be obedient to Christ (1 Peter 1:1-2)* before they can be used for salvation, protection and life.

Just like the hyssop carried the **blood** to the door, our words carry the protection and redemption of *His Blood* today. Words are carriers, and are used, like the hyssop, as a vehicle to transfer the **Blood** from where it was to where it needed to be.

It took the hyssop to transfer the Blood from basin to door. Likewise, it takes words (confession/uttered testimony) to transfer the Blood from the cross to our lives and the lives of others.

Blood means life *(the life is in the **Blood** – Leviticus 17:11).* Yet, that basin was full only of a dead animal's **blood,** and that is all it would have remained, had it not been applied to the door as God had instructed. When applied, the **Blood** protects – *when miss-applied, the Blood is made void.*

Equal to Hyssop

Only after the **blood** was applied, were the benefits secured. Like-wise, only as we apply the **Blood** of Christ will the benefits be secured. Remaining in the basin, the **blood** secured no deliverance. Calvary's **Blood** of 2000 years ago can work no victory nor secure any deliverance until it is brought into the now by our words and applied to the frames of our lives.

Our confessions *(uttered testimonies)* **are equal to the hyssop smearing – they activate and appropriate the Blood.** The **blood** wasn't meant to stay in the basin then, and the **Blood** is not meant to stay in Calvary now. It had to be applied then, and it has to be applied now, otherwise protection will not be appropriated.

The Blood That Required Hyssop Yesterday Requires Our Tongue Today

The riches of the Blood are enjoyed through confessing what that Blood can do. Hyssop was God's only choice for transferring the **blood** back then in Egypt. Today, the words of our mouths are God's method of transfer! No longer is the protection of the **Blood** installed by hyssop, but by our words. The **Blood** required hyssop in Egypt, but requires our words today.

Just Bitter And Small
Until Dripping With The Blood

I cannot over-emphasize *the importance of our uttered testimony.* Let's look at Hebrews chapter 3 verse 1:

*Therefore, holy brothers, who share in the heavenly calling, fix your thoughts on Jesus, the apostle and high priest **whom we confess.***

The writer of Hebrews calls Jesus the High Priest of our confession. The literal meaning of the word *confession* here actually means *saying the same as...* So we must affirm what God says.

Say What God Says

Saying the Same

As believers in Jesus Christ, we need to say the same things with our mouth as God says in His Word. We make the words of our mouths agree with the Word of God.

Our Confession Needs To Be
The Same As His!
Make The Words Of Your Mouth
Agree With His.

Jesus is the High Priest of our confession. Precious saint, realize this sacred truth right here and now with me: **no confession, no High Priest!** Jesus can only advocate on your behalf when you make the right confession.

In plain terms, Jesus, acting as our High Priest, can only effectively support, be an ally to, defend, protect, uphold, cover us and act as our attorney if we are saying the same things He is saying, in obedience to Him *(1 Peter 1:1-2).*

You may call it *Testimony* or you may call it *Confession,* but you can't get away from it. You must confess, you must testify, in accordance with Christ, in order to obtain the salvation protection of Christ.

Jesus said, *By your words you will be justified, and by your words you will be condemned (Matthew 12:37 NKJ).*

You Settle your Destiny by your Words:

James said that your tongue is like the rudder of a ship, it's a very small part of the ship but it determines exactly where the ship will go. It determines the course, path and direction of your life. In other words, ***you will only go where your tongue takes you*** – into obedience or disobedience; heaven or hell.

You Will Only Go Where
Your Own Tongue Takes You

Speak Obedience to Christ

You could even say, ***what your tongue agrees with, is what you will live out.*** If you speak obedience to Christ, you are more likely to live it! If you speak disobedience to Christ, you will live it. What's in the heart will be revealed. If Christ is found there, you will speak Him, and then you will live Him.

We determine the route our lives will take by the way we use our tongues. There is just no way around this. You can say all the right things by agreeing with what is said in the Word of God, or you can say all the wrong things and cause your life to drift off-course.

Whether in your lifetime you eventually find yourself safely at port in the harbor, or whether you remain out at sea shipwrecked, is determined by how you chose to use your tongue.

Destiny Is Determined By How Well You Can Steer Your Ship

Are you really **dying** *to buy that new dress,* or just excited about it? Are you really *tickled to* **death,** or do you just find something funny? Are you truly *starving to* **death,** or are you just a little peckish? How we love to exaggerate. Most of us have used this type of terminology at some point in our lives.

Hopefully, once you've been renewed in your thinking, you've stopped using such terminology. But just see how easy it is to use such a terrible choice of words, when it would have been just as easy not to use them. This world is in such a negative flow. People are far more comfortable using words of death and doom than they are speaking life and joy!

But ultimately you have to understand that you should never say anything that you wouldn't want Jesus (your High Priest) to make happen!

Never underestimate how precious you are to God. Jesus was brutally disfigured when He took our place and was punished instead of us. Did He have any other reason to go to such lengths if we were not precious to Him?

No Cheap Price

The **Blood** of Jesus was not a cheap price to pay, but the Father invested that **Blood** in us. He thought we were worth saving! False humility says that you are to criticize yourself constantly. *What rubbish!* Don't we realize that when we do that, we are really critiquing the One who loved us? How? By touching His workmanship. We are God's handiwork. Let us not even dare to criticize ourselves!

As much as pride is an evil to be routed from the Body of Christ, it is also an evil for us as children of the Most High God to underestimate ourselves – not for anything we have done, but for what God has made us and done through us.

So, to transfer the **Blood** from the basin today is as practical as it was to use the hyssop. We apply the **Blood** *(take it from the basin)* by taking up the words of our mouth in accordance with and in obedience to the Word of God.

By simply acting on what God said, and obeying Him, we bring our words under the **Blood**. Obedience and **Blood** protected the Israelites then, and still protect us now.

The **Blood** works if we obey His word. The first step in obeying His Word is actually **agreeing with it and speaking it.** Then the **Blood** can transform what we say, and what we say can bring deliverance.

The **Blood** only protected them after they had obeyed. To obey is to do what God has said. To do so one has to know what the Word of God is saying. You can't agree with or act upon something you have no knowledge of.

❖

CHAPTER 7

Destiny is in Your Mouth

Our Faith should be Our Profession

Our daily walk in His Word and His Spirit should be what we think about and talk about all the time.

The Just Shall Live By Their Faith

God never does anything without saying it first! God is a faith God. God released His faith in Words, *...Have faith in God (Mark 11:22)*, literally meaning, *Have the God kind of faith or Have the faith of God.*

Ephesians 5:1 literally tells us to be imitators of God, just as children imitate their parents. To imitate God, you must talk like Him and act like Him. He would not ask you to do something you are not capable of doing.

Jesus operated in the faith principles of Mark 11:23 and Matthew 17:20 while He was on earth. He *spoke* to the wind and sea. He *spoke* to demons. He *spoke* to the fig tree. He even *spoke* to dead men!

God Released His Faith In Words

Jesus was imitating His Father and getting the same results. In John 14:12 KJV Jesus said, *...He that believeth on me, the works that I do shall he do also; and greater...* These principles of faith are based on spiritual laws that work for whosoever applies them and sets them in motion by the words that they speak.

If Jesus came to you personally today and said, "As of today, whatsoever you say will directly come to pass, exactly as you have said it," you would appropriate some real quick changes wouldn't you!

Words Are Like Seeds
They Produce After Their Own Kind

Faith comes more quickly when you hear yourself quoting, speaking, and saying the things God said. You will more readily receive God's Word into your spirit by hearing yourself say it than if you hear someone else say it *(Romans 10:17).*

Better Watch what we Say

Much of what the Father supplies to the Body of Christ is *furnished through our confession.* This is not simply our positive, premeditated confession, expressed in prayer, but it consists of *everything* that comes out of our mouths.

Spoken words program our hearts and minds for success or defeat, and our words are the overflow of the condition of our hearts. Christ, as the *High Priest of our confession (Hebrews 3:1),* takes our words, whether in faith or unbelief, and allocates back to us eternal life in proportion to our words.

When our tongue is unbridled, James tells us that our negative confession *...sets on fire the course of our life, and is set on fire by Hell (James 3:6).*

In Hebrews 3:1 we are instructed to:

Consider The Apostle And High Priest Of Our Confession Christ Jesus

The word translated as *profession* in this verse can also be translated as *confession.* God appointed and anointed Jesus to be High Priest over our confessions, or our *...words of faith.*

He is Responsible for bringing our Words to Pass:

1 Corinthians 1:4-5 also tells us that Jesus **enriches** our utterance. That is, He takes our words of faith and enriches them with His Anointing. So, no matter how we look at it, the words we speak carry the very creative force of Almighty God behind them. They will come to pass!

Destiny Is In Your Mouth Be The Prophet Of Your Own Life

We are created to be the *Prophet of our own lives!* Our destiny is in our mouths. It's our words – not everyone else's – that determine our success, or failure, in this life *(Romans*

10:8-9). Our words can bring either good or evil things into our lives.

> *...out of the abundance of the heart **the mouth speaks.** A good man out of the good treasure of his heart brings forth **good things,** and an evil man out of the evil treasure brings forth **evil things.***
>
> (Matthew 12:34-35 NKJ)

Diverse Kinds of Confession

The Confession of Sin *(prior to the Cross):*

Prior to Jesus going to the cross, **John the Baptist and Jesus taught confession of sin to the Jewish people.** The Jews knew what it was to confess their sins and repent, but their sins were only covered in atonement by the **blood** of an animal which was sacrificed once a year.

It wasn't until the sacrifice of Jesus' **Blood** that sin could actually be wiped out and not just covered up *(see Hebrews 10).*

Confession unto Salvation *(after the Cross):*

This is the confession of a sinner, known as the prayer of salvation. In John 16, when Jesus told His disciples about the soon coming Holy Spirit, He explained that the Spirit would come to convict *the world* of sin. But what were these *sinners* to do, once convicted by the Spirit?

Romans 10:8-9 KJV tells us:

> **The word is nigh thee, even in thy mouth,** and in thy heart: that is, the word of faith, which we preach; that if

thou shalt confess with thy mouth the Lord Jesus, and shalt believe in thine heart that God hath raised him from the dead, thou shalt be saved.

Basically, the confession of a sinner under the New Covenant is **Jesus is Lord.**

The Saints' Confession:

Today, the Church is full of Christians who have no idea how to confess their sins once they do step out of fellowship with the Father – which is our third New Testament confession.

The Bible says: if you **have** sin in your life, get it out – confess it, repent of it, get rid of it. Once you do, stand on 1 John 1:9, which says, *If we **confess our sins,** he is faithful and just to forgive us our sins, and to cleanse us from all unrighteousness.*

According to 1 John 1-2, when we as believers are out of fellowship with the Father – that is, when we sin – we know it. That's the time to get rid of it. ***Immediately!*** After all, 1 John 2:1 assures us that, *If any man sin, we have an advocate with the Father, Jesus Christ the righteous.* Don't run from Him when you sin, **run to Him.**

The moment we confessed our sin is the moment we got rid of it. By faith, we *spewed it out* of our mouths, and God was faithful and just to forgive us and cleanse us.

Confession of Our Faith in Christ:

Found in the New Testament is the confession of our faith in God's Word; our faith in Christ *(or His Anointing);*

our faith in God the Father; and our faith in the faithfulness of Jesus as our High Priest.

Remember, whatever you and I receive from God, we receive it by confession.

Your Mouth Is
"The Master Key To Life"

The apostle Paul wrote to the Hebrews:

...Consider The Apostle And
High Priest Of Our Confession Christ Jesus

(Hebrews 3:1)

The word *confession* in the Greek actually means, *saying the same thing as, or saying what God says.*

- It's the affirmation of a Bible truth which you are particularly embracing
- Repeating with your lips, the thing God has said in His Word, which we believe with our heart

What You Feed, You Breed
And What You Starve Dies

A good man eats good from the fruit of his mouth, but the desire of the treacherous is for violence. He who guards his mouth keeps his life, but he who opens wide his lips comes to ruin.

(Proverbs 13:2-3 AMP)

Our confessions – the words we constantly speak day after day – determine all that we will ever receive from God, whether it's salvation, physical healing, peace or financial prosperity. What's more, for the rest of our eternal existence, *this principle of faith working hand in hand with our confession will never change.*

Looking once more at Faith

In Mark 11:23 KJV Jesus explained how the faith process works:

> *Whoever shall* **say** *unto this mountain, Be thou removed, and be thou cast into the sea; and shall not doubt in his heart, but shall believe that those things which he* **saith** *shall come to pass; he shall have whatsoever he* **saith.**

Faith Operates By Believing And Saying And Saying And Saying

Faith operates by believing and saying and saying and saying. It is our confession, or words of faith, that brings possession. In Romans 10:10 we saw that *...With the heart man believeth...and with the mouth confession is made unto...,* and in Matthew 12:34-35 *...Out of the abundance of the heart the mouth speaketh...*

We lay hold of the word by receiving it by faith, and then *confessing* it. **This same process got us saved and it's this process that will get us anything else God has promised!** Remember, once we lay hold of the promises of God with our faith and our confession, that's when Jesus' enriching anointing and ministry come into play.

That's why the Apostle Paul told Timothy that *words of faith* nourish, but idle words starve the spirit and make it weak *(1 Timothy 4:6-7).*

So, we must *hold fast the profession of our faith...* because it is our **confession** of faith which makes the difference between life or death.

❖

CHAPTER 8

Seven Divine Legacies

Revealed in the New Testament are seven major ways by which the **Blood** of Jesus works for us.

*In him we have redemption through his **Blood**.*
(Ephesians 1:7)

1. REDEMPTION

We have redemption through His **Blood.** Redemption means to be *bought back.* We were in the hands of the Devil and Jesus bought us back with His **Blood.**

*For you know that it was not with perishable things such as silver or gold that you were redeemed from the empty way of life handed down to you from your forefathers, but with the precious **Blood** of Christ, a lamb without blemish or defect.*

(1 Peter 1:18-19)

The mention that is made of the lamb only takes us back once more to the Passover. Jesus was without blemish, spot, original or personal sin, and we have been redeemed by His **Blood.**

The Redeemed Must Say So

In the same context we read in Psalm 107:2 KJV:

> **Let the redeemed of the Lord SAY SO,** *whom he hath redeemed from the hand of the enemy.*

Who is the enemy? Satan. And if we are redeemed, what do we have to do about it? **Say so!** *You must understand that if there is no say so, there can be no redemption.* It's your testimony that makes it work for you. Otherwise the **blood** stays in the basin.

2. CLEANSING

The Blood does not cleanse in the Dark:

> **IF we** [really] **are living and walking in the Light,** *as He* [Himself] *is in the Light, we have* [true, unbroken] *fellowship with one another, and* **the Blood of Jesus Christ His Son cleanses** (removes) **us from all sin** *and guilt* [keeps us cleansed from sin in all its forms and manifestations].
> *(1 John 1:7 AMP)*

Please note that **the evidence that you are walking in the light is that you have fellowship. And if you get out of fellowship, you get out of the light, and if you get out of the light, the Blood does not cleanse in the dark.**

If we continue walking in the light, we continue having fellowship one with another, and Jesus His Son continually cleanses us from all sin. It's a *continual provision,* no matter where we are. If we are in the light – regardless of the diverse circumstances that we may be encountering – as long as we are continuing in the light Jesus is cleansing us of **all** sin.

Psalm 51:7 KJV says, *Purge me with hyssop, and I shall be clean: wash me, and I shall be whiter than snow.* Notice the use of hyssop. What was he thinking of? **The Passover – that's right!**

What a privilege it is to know where to go when we are guilty! We all have that privilege, praise the Lord. But just think of the billions of precious people who are guilty and don't know where they can go.

Imagine for one moment again the torment of a guilty conscience; endlessly agonizing over the reality of your sin and not having any knowledge of where you could go to find the forgiveness and peace you need. Sadly, this describes the condition of a large percentage of humanity today!

We Are Required To Stay In The Light To Enjoy The Protection Of The Blood

If we walk in the **Light,** His **Blood** will cleanse us continually from all sin. But we have to walk in the light – just like the Israelites had to be inside their homes and not outside.

No excuses! No popping over to the corner shop that night of the Passover, nor visiting a friend, not even taking a breath of fresh air in the back garden! They were commanded to stay indoors; and to venture outside, regardless of the reason, would have caused their own death.

Likewise, we have to stay in the **Light** and be obedient not to stray from it, then *the Blood remains our surety.*

3. JUSTIFICATION

Justification is yet another provision and the Greek translation basically means *to make righteous,* although it also has many other shades of meaning.

If we take a look at Romans 5:9 in the Amplified Bible it tells us, *Therefore, since* **we are Now justified** *(acquitted, made righteous, and brought into right relationship with God)* **by Christ's Blood,** *how much more [certain is it that] we shall be saved by Him from the indignation and wrath of God.*

We are justified **now** because of the **Blood.** Let's take an example. Imagine you are on trial for a capital offense and the verdict comes out *Not guilty.* That means you have been *acquitted,* and even more, you have been *reckoned righteous,* with the righteousness of Jesus Christ – **not** your own, but His. It also means that you have been **made** righteous.

So, in the different shades of its meaning, *to be justified* means:

- not guilty
- acquitted
- reckoned righteous
- made righteous

Then one can actually say, *I have been made righteous. I am justified,* which means I can stand before God **just as if I had never sinned!**

Justified
Just As If I Had Never Sinned

How can you say such a thing? Because I have been made righteous with the righteousness of Jesus Christ and **He never sinned. He had no guilt and no past to cover up.**

No other righteousness than the righteousness of Jesus Christ can stand justified before God. No one will enter heaven with his or her own righteousness; it has to be the righteousness of Christ. Filthy rags won't get your passage through those pearly gates – only the **Blood**-washed robes can do it!

Ditch the filthy rags and allow the impartation of His **Blood** to make you righteous – giving the devil no right to accuse you any longer.

Isaiah 61:10-11 AMP says:

> *I will greatly rejoice in the Lord, my soul will exult in my God; for He has clothed me with the garments of salvation,* **He has covered me with the robe of righteousness...** *so [surely] the Lord God will cause righteousness and justice and praise to spring forth before all the nations [through the self-fulfilling power of His word].*

If you trust the Lord Jesus and His sacrifice, which He made for you, then He will surely clothe you with salvation.

But you must never stop there, for He also wants to robe you with His righteousness, literally to cover or wrap you around with it! You are literally covered from head to toe and in every way possible with the righteousness of Christ Jesus.

And all this of course means that the Accuser has nothing left to say against us. If he tries – simply agree! *What?* That's right, agree! Just say, *You're quite right Satan, but all of that is in my past and now I am clothed in the righteousness of Jesus Christ. Let's see what you can find wrong with that!*

So, let the redeemed of the Lord **Say So.** Open your mouth and declare:

Through the Blood of Jesus I am justified, acquitted,

not guilty, reckoned righteous, just as if I'd never sinned.

Thank You, Jesus!

4. SANCTIFICATION

*Therefore Jesus also, that he might **sanctify** the people with his own blood, suffered outside the gate.*
                                                    (Hebrews 13:12 NKJ)

To sanctify in the original is directly related to holiness. Actually, the word *sanct* is the same word we use in English for *saint,* so to sanctify is to make saintly or to make holy. It has two aspects: one is negative – we are set apart from sin and everything that defiles, and the second is positive as we are then made holy with God's own holiness.

God's Chastisement:

> *For [our earthly fathers] disciplined us for only a short period of time and **chastised** us as seemed proper and good to them; but He disciplines us for our certain good, that we may become **sharers in His own holiness.***
>
> *(Hebrews 12:10 AMP)*

Notice it is **Not Our** holiness any more than **Our** righteousness, but **His** holiness. How do we partake in His holiness? Through the **Blood** of Jesus.

Now again, let the redeemed of the Lord **Say So.** Saying it is applying it. We take it unto ourselves by believing it in our hearts and confessing it with our mouths, the same way we appropriated salvation. The word of God is the power of God unto salvation to those who **believe.**

We must believe it and confess it. So here goes, shout it from the roof tops:

Through the Blood of Jesus I am:

- sanctified
- made holy
- set apart to God
- separated from sin
- made holy, with God's own holiness

You must understand that when we are saying these things out loud as a confession of the heart, we are dipping the hyssop into the basin and sprinkling the Blood over ourselves!

5. LIFE

Some people have the idea that all the provisions made by the **Blood** of Jesus were only negative, deriving that the **Blood** only ever saved us **from** something. But in response to such folly we could remind them that **Jesus' life was in His Blood** and there is nothing more positive than **Life!**

> *...the life of the flesh is in the blood,* and I have given it to you upon the altar to make atonement for your souls; for *it is the blood that makes atonement* for the soul.
> *(Leviticus 17:11 NKJ)*

So, the very **Life of God** Himself is in the **Blood** of Jesus! His very own life, the life of the **Creator!** Our human minds have no way to calculate the potential of that statement because the Creator is infinitely greater than **all** that He has created. The entire created universe is just a snap of His fingers.

Oh, if we could truly grasp what there is for us in that precious **Blood!**

Derek Prince is quoted to have said:

> *"There is more life in just one single drop of the Blood of Jesus than there is in the entire kingdom of Satan."*

This can be said because we've got the eternal, uncreated, measureless life of God Himself, a life that existed before anything else was ever created – and it is all in the **Blood of Jesus!**

And Jesus said to them, I assure you, **most solemnly I tell you, you cannot have any life in you unless you eat the flesh of the Son of Man and drink His Blood** *[unless you* **appropriate** *His life and the saving merit of His* **Blood**].

He who feeds on My flesh and drinks My **Blood** *has (possesses now) eternal life, and I will raise him up [from the dead] on the last day.*

For My flesh is true and genuine food, and My **Blood** *is true and genuine drink. He who feeds on My flesh and drinks My* **Blood dwells continually** *in Me, and I [in like manner dwell continually] in him.*

Just as the living Father sent Me and I live by (through, because of) the Father, even so whoever **continues to feed** *on Me [whoever takes Me for his food and is nourished by Me] shall [in his turn] live through and because of Me.*
(John 6:53-57 AMP)

The word *appropriate* literally means to **take possession of; take to oneself.** Its other shades of meaning include: *adopt, seize, secure, take in, apply, fitting.*

We are to seize all that the **Blood** gained for us and not be slack in doing so because **Jesus truly made every provision for us, through His precious Blood.**

Now, when we take communion, we are literally eating His flesh and drinking His **Blood!** This is a stumbling block for many – and yet an unavoidable truth. Even those present at the time when Jesus made these statements, couldn't handle what He was saying, and many still find it hard to swallow now.

Yet, the fact remains that we remember His **Blood** by participating in the eating of His flesh and the drinking of His **Blood.**

There may be various ways to apply this truth contained in John 6, but for me and my family, we literally eat and drink Jesus! For many the communion is merely seen as a memorial – but that was not what Jesus said. He said it the only way it can be said:

You Are Eating My Flesh And Drinking My Blood!

Sure, we are doing it in memorial to, but that's not *"it"* – we are partaking in the actual Body and **Blood** of Christ. *There's no reason to change those words.*

Then there are many differing arguments and opinions as to how the communion becomes the Body and the **Blood.** For instance, the Catholics and liturgical churches believe it's through consecration by a priest. Personally, that's not the belief I hold.

I believe it *becomes* **the Body and the Blood through Faith!** When I receive it in **Faith,** believing what Jesus said in His Word, it becomes to me precisely what He said it would be: **His Body and His Blood!**

> *The cup of blessing [of wine at the Lord's Supper] upon which we ask [God's] blessing, does it not mean [that in drinking it] we **participate in and share** a fellowship (a communion) in **the Blood of Christ** (the Messiah)?*

The bread which we break, does it not mean [that in eating it] **we participate in and share** *a fellowship (a communion) in* **the body of Christ?**
(1 Corinthians 10:16 AMP)

For I received from the Lord Himself that which I passed on to you [it was given to me personally], that the Lord Jesus on the night when He was treacherously delivered up and while His betrayal was in progress took bread, and when He had given thanks, He broke [it] and said, **Take, eat. This is My body,** *which is broken for you. Do this to call Me [affectionately] to remembrance.*
(1 Corinthians 11:23-24 AMP)

Now it's **perfectly true that we do this** *in remembrance of Him,* yet, what are we doing to remember Him? We are partaking in **His Body!**

Similarly when supper was ended, He took the cup also, saying, This cup is the new covenant [ratified and established] in **My Blood.** *Do this, as often as you drink [it], to call me [affectionately] to remembrance.*

For **every time** *you eat this bread and drink this cup,* **you are representing and signifying and proclaiming the fact of the Lord's death until He comes [again].**

So then whoever eats the bread or drinks the cup of the Lord in a way that is unworthy [of Him] will be guilty of [profaning and sinning against] **the body and the Blood of the Lord.**
(1 Corinthians 11:25-27 AMP)

We have no past but the cross, and no future but His coming, and we proclaim His death until He comes again. Every time we do it [communion] we remind ourselves that He's coming again!

To appropriate this you could say:

Lord Jesus, I gladly receive Your Blood

And the life that's within it, the very life of God

Infinite and eternal life

Thank You, Lord!

Paul said, in due course death will be swallowed up by life – the decay of our natural bodies can be swallowed up by the very life of God – on a daily basis!

Paul said that though our outward man be wasting away, our inward man is renewed day by day and ***there's enough life in the inward man to keep our outward man alive until our task is finished. Hallelujah!*** *(2 Corinthians 4:16)*

6. INTERCESSION

*...Jesus, the Mediator (Go-between, Agent) of a new covenant and to **the sprinkled Blood which speaks [of mercy]**, a better and nobler and more gracious message than the blood of Abel [which cried out for vengeance].*
(Hebrews 12:24 AMP)

Three Main Contrasting Elements:

- Abel's blood was shed against his will
  Jesus willingly Gave His Blood

- Abel's blood was sprinkled on earth
  Jesus' Blood was sprinkled in the Holiest of all

- Abel's blood called out for vengeance
  Jesus' Blood cried out for mercy

It's always very precious to remember that the **Blood** of Jesus has been sprinkled in the **immediate presence** of Almighty God and is speaking on our behalf – crying out for **Mercy.**

To appropriate this truth you could **Say** *(confess/take possession of):*

Jesus... Thank you!

In those times I pray amiss...

Your Blood still cries out for me.

7. ACCESS

*Therefore, brethren, having **boldness** to enter the Holy Place by the **Blood** of Jesus, by a new and living way which he consecrated for us, through the veil, that is, his flesh, and having a high priest over the house of God, let us draw near with a true heart in **full assurance** of faith, having our hearts **sprinkled** from an evil conscience and our bodies washed with pure water.*

*Let us **hold fast the confession** of our hope without wavering, for he who promised is faithful.*
(Hebrews 10:19-23 NKJ)

The word *boldness* used here means *freedom of speech.* It's very important that our **boldness** gives us freedom of speech. **Remember, it is our testimony –** *if we don't testify – we don't have it!*

Then we must pay particular attention to verse 23 where it tells us to *...**hold fast** the confession of our hope without wavering (also in Hebrews 4:14).* No matter how much turbulence you have, you must keep a fast hold and don't let go. **Keep on keeping on!** Continue making the right confession, regardless of all contrary circumstances. Why? Because God's word is true!

We can approach the throne of Almighty God and the holiest place in the universe in complete **boldness** and assurance of faith, because of the **Blood** of Jesus. **We have been given unlimited access!**

Once again **we have to** *Say It.* **So open your mouth now and declare:**

Thank You, Father

That through the sprinkled Blood of Jesus

Boldness and access belong to me

I have legal entry

Into Your immediate presence

In the Holiest Place of all

In summary, the **Seven Provisions** of the **Blood** are:

- Redemption
- Cleansing
- Justification

- Sanctification
- Life
- Intercession
- Access

The Blood was sprinkled seven times and continues to work within us seven different ways.

However, we must never forget that, notwithstanding all the provisions of the **Blood,** it is still **The Blood** *and* **Our Testimony** that wins the victory. Therefore, let our final declaration be:

We overcome Satan because of the BLOOD

by

SAYING what that BLOOD did for us

but

Neither do we shrink from death

but we

Take up our cross daily and follow Christ

In order to die to the things of the flesh

(Revelation 12:11; Luke 14:26-27)

❖

Summary

The Heart of the message in *His Life Is In The Blood*

Blood is the trophy of every battle – and for Jesus, His spilt Blood was His trophy, and ours. That Blood helps us today; it's our freedom from sin and bondage. Nothing can enter the Blood-bought Temples of the Holy Ghost that we are today!

However, the lamb of the Old Testament didn't just lend his blood; it had to be applied to the doorframes – with hyssop. Just a symbolic gesture, or a very crucial step towards freedom? *(Today we apply the Blood of Jesus not with hyssop, but with our tongues.)*

This book will encourage you to apply the Blood of the Passover Lamb, Jesus Christ, to your life, just as the children of Israel did in the Old Testament. Not merely talking or reading about it, but applying it.

Imagine if they had failed – they would have perished. And if we fail to apply and appropriate the Blood in our day

– we will perish also! Let's be intelligent about the Blood. The fathers of Israel might have believed that Moses heard from God, even though it sounded crazy to apply blood with a bitter herb to their front doors. But unless they acted upon what they believed, it would not have worked for them.

Consider this: there had to be a hearing and a doing of God's Word, which also required obedience! In our day and age of increasing insecurity, we had better know how to appropriate the blessed Blood of the Lamb to the doorframes of our lives – not out of fear but faith – believing what the final book says when it states:

They OVERCAME him

By the BLOOD of the Lamb

And by the WORD of their TESTIMONY

Revelation 12:11

Forward or Pass it On!

Note: If this book has blessed you, let it bless others. Share it, and let the message bear fruit in someone else's life. *"What you have heard... entrust to... others"* (2 Timothy 2:2). Why not sow by gifting a copy, or even placing a bundle in the hands of your home group or church? In this way the truth multiplies and glorifies our Heavenly Father.

A massive Thank You

❖

Bibliography

- Andrews, Ian. <u>Building a People of Power</u>. Published by Word Publishing, Word (UK) Ltd. Printed in UK.

- Basansky, Bill. <u>Life & Power of the Blood Covenant</u>. Published by Harrison House. Printed in USA.

- Conner, Kevin J. <u>The Feasts of Israel</u>. Published by Bible Temple Publishing. Printed in USA.

- Kenyon, E.W. <u>The Blood Covenant</u>. Copyright © 1999. Published by Kenyon's Gospel Publishing Society. Printed in USA.

- Morgan, G. Campbell and Charles H. Spurgeon. <u>Understanding the Holy Spirit</u>. Copyright © 1995. Published by AMG Publishers. Printed in USA.

- Strong, James. S.T.D., L.L.D. 1890. <u>Strong's Exhaustive Concordance; Dictionaries of the Hebrew and Greek Words</u>. e-Sword® version 7.6.1 Copyright © 2000-2005. All Rights Reserved. Registered trade mark of Rick Meyers. Equipping Ministries Foundation. USA www.e-sword.net.

- <u>Wikipedia</u>: The Largest Online Research Site and Encyclopedia www.wikipedia.org. Found under "Saddam Hussein."

Drs Alan and Jennifer Pateman

Senior and Co-Apostles

Drs Alan and Jennifer Pateman, missionaries
from the UK, who at present reside in Tuscany, Italy,
and travel together as an apostolic couple. They
are the Founders of Alan Pateman World Missions,
Connecting for Excellence International,
and LifeStyle International Christian University.
President and Vice President of
World Missions Ministries Association
and APMI Publishing/Publications.

*(Please see our website for all profile and
international information, itinerant, conferences
and graduations, etc.)*

www.AlanPatemanWorldMissions.com

❖

To Contact the Author

Please email:

Alan Pateman World Missions

Email: apostledr@alanpatemanworldmissions.com
Web: www.AlanPatemanWorldMissions.com

*Please include your prayer requests
and comments when you write.*

❖

Other Books

Forgiveness, The Key to Revival

Scripture is absolute when it comes to forgiveness. IF we forgive, THEN we are forgiven. It's that simple but no one said it was easy! Nonetheless, forgiveness can be likened to a spiritual key that unlocks spiritual doors and opportunities!

ISBN: 978-1-909132-41-2, Pages: 124, Format: Paperback, Published: 2013
Also available in eBook format!

Why War: A Biblical Approach to the Armour of God and Spiritual Warfare

Spiritual warfare means different things to different people, but from a biblical standpoint Ephesians 6:10-18 gives us the best biblical definition of spiritual warfare possible. We can also see how God has thoroughly equipped us for victory not just self defence!

ISBN: 978-1-909132-39-9, Pages: 180, Format: Paperback, Published: 2013
Also available in eBook format!

All Books Available

at

APMI PUBLICATIONS

Email: publications@alanpatemanworldmissions.com
*Also Available from Amazon.com
and other retail outlets.*

*If you purchased this book through Amazon.com
or other and enjoyed reading it, or perhaps one of
my other books, I would be grateful if you could
take a couple of minutes to write a Customer
Review, many thanks.*

By Dr. Alan Pateman

By Dr. Jennifer Pateman

Available from APMI Publications, Amazon.com and Other Retail Outlets

www.ingramcontent.com/pod-product-compliance
Lightning Source LLC
Chambersburg PA
CBHW071549040426

42452CB00008B/1124